Disputing the Dead

Disputing the Dead

*U.S. Law on
Aboriginal Remains
and Grave Goods*

H. Marcus Price III

University of Missouri Press
Columbia and London

Library of Congress Cataloging-in-Publication Data
Price, H. Marcus, 1943–
    Disputing the dead : U.S. law on aboriginal remains and
grave goods / H. Marcus Price III.
        p.   cm.
    Includes bibliographical references.
    ISBN 0–8262–0779–0
    1. Indians of North America—Antiquities—Law and
legislation. 2. Exhumation—Law and legislation—United
States. 3. Cemeteries—Law and legislation—United States.
4. Indians of North America—Mortuary customs. I. Title.
KF8210.A57P75   1991
346.7301′3—dc20
[347.30613]   90–29185
                                                                   CIP

∞™ This paper meets the minimum requirements of
the American National Standard for Permanence of Paper
for Printed Library Materials, Z39.48, 1984.

Designer: Rhonda Gibson
Typesetter: Connell-Zeko Type & Graphics
Printer: Thomson-Shore, Inc.
Binder: Thomson-Shore, Inc.
Typeface: Dutch

To Linda

Contents

Acknowledgments

Mid-life changes in life-style and location and a new obligation to take up an unfamiliar career are traumatic burdens for anyone to assume. When these sacrifices are undertaken cheerfully to support the pursuit of ill-understood and non-remunerative interests held by another, great love and selflessness are at play. I will be forever grateful for the support and counsel of my wife, Linda, during the course of my research and the preparation of this manuscript.

Broad efforts of the sort represented by this book rest on the shoulders of those who have prepared previous surveys. This study stands on the foundations provided by certain scholars. I especially want to recognize the work of Lawrence Rosen (who wrote what is probably the seminal article on the issue), Brona Simon and Valerie Talmage, Douglas Ubelaker and Lauryn Grant, Steve Moore, Margaret Bowman, Dean Higginbotham, Walter Echo-Hawk, Paul Wilson, and Elaine Zingg.

I acknowledge the many individuals who provided assistance in the preparation of this study. Very special support was given by several, including Larry Zimmerman, Lynne Goldstein, Nancy Lurie, and Michael J. Fox (recently of the Heard Museum). Finally, I thank a most thorough and generous attorney and anthropologist in Albuquerque, Michael H. Schneider, who freely offered me the benefit of the results of several years of research he had invested in aspects of this topic. My thanks to you all.

Disputing the Dead

1   Introduction

You have to treat this [disposition of prehistoric aboriginal remains] in a respectful manner. I think that's the most highlighted thing of this reburial issue. That it has to be treated in a respectful manner. It has to be treated in a respectful manner.

Weldon Johnson
Assistant Director of the Colorado River
Indian Tribal Museum and Representative
of the Intertribal Council of Arizona

Weldon Johnson's simple, sensible statement cloaks an issue that elicits strong emotion and diverse, often contradictory, opinion. Few parties involved in the controversy surrounding appropriate disposition of prehistoric aboriginal[1] remains and grave goods would take exception to Weldon Johnson's position. But "respect" is a subjective, value-laden term.

The potential for conflict is substantial. Although the exact figure is impossible to determine, we may estimate conservatively that the remains of at least several hundred precontact aborigines, many with associated grave goods, are discovered annually. In addition, collections currently held by museums, historical societies, universities, and private collectors include the remains of as many as 600,000 individuals (Preston 1989:67).

For many members of the aboriginal communities, these remains are symbols of spiritual and political power. For members of the scientific and museological communities, human remains yield data that can advance our understanding of human variation and evolution, thus benefiting all of humanity. Moreover, scientists and museologists engaged in the study and preservation of remains also base a significant portion of their livelihood on these activities.

1. Throughout this study the term "aboriginal" is employed to designate both native Indian and native Hawaiian populations. "Indian," of course, applies only to American Indians. The expression "native American" is avoided whenever possible because of its imprecision (Gill 1983:144).

1

There is considerable diversity of opinion about what constitutes respectful treatment of prehistoric aboriginal remains and grave goods, even among members of the same community. Among the scientific community, Brace (1988:3) suggests that in light of the lack of knowledge regarding mortuary preferences of prehistoric aboriginal populations and uncertainty over the validity of claims presented by living aboriginal individuals, museum custody might be the most appropriate way of honoring the remains. Hanson (1989:1) considers scientific examination of remains one of the highest forms of respect. Meighan (1984:217–19; 1986:6–7, 13) supports this view, especially as prehistoric mortuary preferences are not necessarily compatible with extant aboriginal preferences. Zimmerman (1985a:11; 1985b), in contrast, offers the possibility of compromise with contemporary aboriginal groups on the issue and argues that the scientific community will realize important benefits from such a compromise. Walker (1989:5) considers the wishes of living aboriginal Americans to have ethical and moral priority over any right of museologists or archaeologists (and presumably physical anthropologists) to study or display aboriginal dead.

Among the aboriginal community, Johnson (Quick 1985:21) implies that decisions pertaining to respectful disposition of remains should be dealt with on an ad hoc basis because beliefs among tribes about exhumation vary; he cites the example of the Mojave, who consider treatment of postcremation remains to be of little significance. Jan Hammil presents a different nuance of this position by insisting that aboriginal groups have ultimate control over the disposition of all prehistoric aboriginal remains and grave goods (Quick 1985:46, 52), though this does not necessarily preclude scientific examination of the remains. Other Indian groups (such as American Indians Against Desecration) reportedly insist that all archaeology is desecration and that all prehistoric aboriginal remains and grave goods should be immediately returned to Indian communities for ceremonial disposition (Meighan 1984:210–11; Brookes 1988:21; Ubelaker and Grant 1989:254).

Representatives of some aboriginal groups demand authority over the disposition of the remains and associated grave goods of decedents whom they allege to be their ancestors. Some members of the academic and museological communities resist these claims when the deceased individual cannot be identified and the aboriginal claimants cannot establish direct familial affinity with the deceased. Recourse to the courts and to the legislature is increasingly sought to resolve the disputes.

The United States is comprised of numerous communities formed along lines of economic, power, gender, and ethnic criteria, among many others. Various communities and even individuals within single communities may have different opinions—reflecting different "values"—about the treatment of aboriginal remains. Culture is a complex repertoire of values (Goodenough 1964:11–12; Kay 1966:106), and the cultural dynamics pertinent to both shared and conflicting values results in formal law. At any given time some of these values are dormant and some are active, and no individual member of a culture is aware of or possesses the full repertoire of potential values held by the culture (Roberts 1964: 438–41). The confluence of value systems that arise from different communities within a larger culture regarding a specific issue will shape that culture's formal law on the issue. So it is in the United States with the question of appropriate treatment of aboriginal remains and grave goods.

Law is a phenomenon of culture and reflects norms of behavioral values (there is some argument, however, that law may be out of phase with those norms) held by the host culture (Bohannon 1965:37; Hoebel 1954:15; Nader 1965:17). Law does not exist independently of those values (Fineman 1986:781). It assumes substance and form only in the context of the ordering of specific relationships between individuals, though in a given relationship this ordering may take the form of indirect influence through normative ideals rather than direct intervention by legal institutions.

An extensive body of literature debates which definition of law is the most powerful and parsimonious for the study of law in a social science context, and whether a universal definition of law is possible. The competing views are exhaustively summarized by Nader (1965), Pospisil (1968), and Starr and Collier (1987), among others. When the term *law* is employed in this study, I refer to formal law in general and usually to formal law in the United States.

A multiplicity of sometimes contradictory legal solutions to a problem suggests that the host culture has not resolved the priorities for competing values into a modal ordering. This study addresses formal law at the state and federal levels. Inconsistent laws between the various states may imply that the modal ordering of values differs among states, or that the modal priorities are unresolved in each state, or that the laws implemented to protect modal priorities are new and untested as to effect on competing values—or that some combination of these three possibilities has occurred.

Variation in laws may be expected here, where the values at issue compete with other values—as in private ownership of property, separation of church and state, and advancement of scientific knowledge—and where a modal balance between competing values has not been established. Indeed, it is clear that while the modal values of the citizenry of the United States appear to dictate respectful treatment of human remains (Echo-Hawk 1988:2), the constituent elements of that respect remain unresolved (Zimmerman 1985a) and the laws pertaining to it are in an evolutionary state (Echo-Hawk 1985:1; Wilson and Zingg 1974:45). Most legislation specifically addressing the issue is relatively new and has not been tested against competing values that it will affect.

Legislated solutions take many forms. Often specific laws enacted to address the issue are in a state of flux and are subject to progressive modification. In 1989 at least nine items of federal legislation, either new or modifications of existing laws, were presented to Congress on different aspects of the issue (Funk 1989), and at least eleven states considered such legislation pertaining to aboriginal remains. Sometimes the proposed laws have been inconsistent with one another, and frequently new laws have conflicted or overlapped with preexisting legislation in the same jurisdiction.

All states address the issue through law. Accounts sometimes are published of the number of states that have specific "unmarked burial" legislation (see, for example, anon. 1989a:2, which cites nineteen states, and Tomsho 1989:A11, which notes twenty). These are generally misleading reports and in the context of comparisons of applicable state laws, too narrowly restrict the laws to be considered. Many states, such as Alabama, Kentucky, and Texas, apply their general public health and sepulchral laws to prehistoric aboriginal remains in the absence of particular legislation, and even in states enjoying specific legislation, the laws often operate in tandem with general laws, as in Alaska and Virginia. Thus, to understand how individual states deal in legal terms with the issue, it is necessary to compare the applicable legal regime of every state, not merely those of states possessing legislation specific to the issue.

The Study of Ethnic Conflict

Ethnic conflict is a powerful force shaping human affairs. The significance of such conflict is underscored by the argument that democracy cannot survive in the face of serious ethnic division (Horowitz 1985:xi, 681). Aboriginal populations in the United States are in a state of social and cultural transition, and often they are in conflict with European-

American society. This phenomenon is commonly considered a variant of revitalization (Gill 1983:144–73; Marx 1973:163; Walker 1972:739, 745; Zimmerman 1981:10). Lurie (1971a:194–95) and others observe that the modern aboriginal social dynamic is so distinct as to constitute a new order of cultural phenomenon. Lurie distinguishes this phenomenon from classical revitalization by labeling it "renascence," for reasons discussed in the next chapter. Significant features of the process include newly developing pan-Indian definitions of sacredness (Zimmerman 1985b:1) and the focus of the aboriginal community on formal law, specifically law pertaining to the disposition of prehistoric aboriginal remains and grave goods (Higginbotham 1982:92).

This aboriginal social dynamic—entailing interethnic conflict, processes of enculturation, and possibly the creation of tradition and new ethnic identity—invites coordinated study from a variety of perspectives. As the aboriginal social movement relies heavily on formal law, including that which bears on the disposition of human remains and grave goods, and as formal law is a public and usually published forum, several interdisciplinary studies oriented around the formal legal issues should provide insight into the dynamics of ethnic interaction. In such an investigation, an essential perspective would emerge from a historical chronicle recording the major events, dates, and players in the aboriginal condition in the United States. Another avenue of inquiry would be a political analysis of relevant polities (federal, state, tribal, and local) and the stresses and relationships among them. Some professionals (Heizer 1974; Trigger 1986) suggest a third approach aimed at professional ethical responsibility: What is the appropriate ethical response by professional scholars and administrators to aboriginal requests for repatriation and disposition of aboriginal remains and grave goods?

The dynamics of aboriginal social movement also provide a useful model for studying a variety of social processes: the formation of values and modal ordering of priorities among competing values within the same social group and between different groups; the effect of power differentials among individual groups within American society and different strategies employed by them; the creation and exploitation of networks among aboriginal populations; the impact of advances in communication and transportation technology on social movements; the various modes of interethnic dispute resolution employed by the disputants; and the processes that create an ethnic identity (pan-Indian) and tradition where none existed historically.

Collier (1975) and Comaroff and Roberts (1981), among others, have provided a useful "umbrella" research design. Their processual approach is related to broader theories of symbolic interactionism, transactional analysis, and game theory. This approach concentrates on the social context of law. Disputes are not considered discrete, bounded events, but rather part of the greater social "flow" (Comaroff and Roberts 1981: 3–22), and specialized legal institutions are viewed as one interrelated element of the greater societal framework (Starr and Collier 1987:371).

Study of interethnic conflict should begin at the point where the players most clearly and openly interact (Barth 1981:83). Formal law, as noted earlier, can be an unusually public forum for the resolution of conflict between ethnic groups and their respective values. Records of those involved and their arguments and objectives are readily accessible to the student. In the dynamics of contemporary aboriginal confrontation with European-American society, one useful starting point for observation is the issue of appropriate disposition of aboriginal remains and grave goods. Formal law—specifically the legal issue of appropriate disposition of prehistoric aboriginal remains and grave goods—is a primary element in the contemporary aboriginal social dynamic. Thus, study centered around formal laws and legal processes should give insight into other social processes in the dynamic.

However, an integral part of the data base required to pursue these studies remains to be established. The primary purpose of this study is to analyze for the first time all state and federal laws in the United States pertaining to the disposition of prehistoric aboriginal remains and grave goods.

The Methods

After reviewing both the literature pertaining to aboriginal remains and grave goods as well as relevant federal and state laws, I have had my own review of the statutes cross-checked through the Lexis and Westlaw computerized data bases. To assess the various laws in practice, I then solicited the advice and opinions of every state attorney general and state historic preservation officer. I also sought assistance from major federal agencies and state archaeologists, and for aboriginal perspectives, approached the Native American Rights Fund and representatives of tribal groups in several states.

In all, several hundred archaeologists, educators, museologists, aboriginal representatives, physical anthropologists, and legal counsel were queried. My investigation has led to an informative relationship with the national task force for the study of the issue sponsored by the Society for American Archaeology, an appointment to the American Anthropological Association Commission on Native American Reburial, and an invitation to participate in the National Dialogue on Museum–Native American Relations conducted by the Heard Museum in Phoenix, Arizona. These activities have provided insight into considerations for the creation of national policies on the topic. In addition, I was fortunate to cochair a panel on law and politics concerning this issue at the World Archaeological Congress held in August 1989, an activity that contributed greatly to my understanding of the global aboriginal social process.

This study is as complete and accurate as possible, with qualifications. It can only be employed as a social science resource that provides patterns and relative conclusions at law for a given time. It is not a substitute for the advice of legal counsel trained and experienced in the jurisdiction in which a particular problem might arise. However, it should prove valuable as a point from which to commence the study of laws in a specific jurisdiction.

As will be seen, this is a dynamic area of law, experiencing constant and rapid change. An arbitrary cutoff date for discussion of state laws had to be established in order to bring the research to a close for publication. In general this cutoff date is August 1989, though there are some subsequent revisions and additions. Because there is less material, it was possible to make discussion of federal legislation current through December 1990. Ultimately, laws of a specific jurisdiction that are of special interest must be individually researched in order to accurately determine the current treatment at law of the issue in that jurisdiction.

Several of the statutes described below are presently under challenge at court on federal and state constitutional grounds. Furthermore, statutory law is always subject to judicial interpretation that might alter the otherwise apparent effect of the statutory text in a given situation. Local county and city ordinances may also affect the impact of the statutory text when remains and grave goods are discovered within the boundaries of such polities.

The somewhat uneven treatment of the various states is due, in part, to differences in response from the states and to differences regarding the urgency of, and consequent attention to, the issue. Typically, less attention to the matter results from a lack of significant local aboriginal presence or absence of known archaeological remains. To a large degree, relevant data remain unpublished and available only through informal channels. As one expects with an emotionally charged issue, some of the informants have political agendas, and bias in reporting is a constant risk.

2 Apparent Social Patterns and the Law

Law exists only in a social context. Knowledge of the history and cultural foundation of the values at play aids in understanding the nature and genesis of the strategies at law employed to implement those values. As stated in the Introduction, this study does not constitute a thorough analysis of the contemporary aboriginal social dynamic in the United States, though the data used here may contribute to such an analysis. Nevertheless, certain preliminary patterns appear in the literature and are suggested by the data. Accordingly, with some reluctance and a note of caution, those apparent patterns are discussed below.

The nature of the contemporary aboriginal social process is complex and obscure and is related to revitalization movements. Speaking in broad terms, classic revitalization is a deliberate, organized attempt by some members of a society to construct a more satisfying culture by rapid acceptance of a pattern of multiple innovations. Although such a movement may be precipitated by a variety of causes, the most common is the perception by a population of subordination and inferiority with respect to an adjacent society (Wallace 1970:188–89).

Wallace (1970:192–99) describes the mechanics of revitalization as an emergence of a charismatic leader or a nuclear interest group that establishes an ideal or "goal" format for a new society. This goal is communicated to other members of the society, often with religious elements (Worsely 1959:126), although these may be innovations and not reflections of traditional religions (Dobyns and Euler 1967:viii). This is followed by the organization of converts and the adaptation of the goal to the needs and wishes of the greater body of adherents.

American aborigines, especially Indians, have long been associated with revitalization movements. Most of the literature addressing the revitalization process in ethnic groups in the United States pertains to Indians. The present pan-Indian movement is especially complex, involving a broad variety of ethnic groups, and is in a dynamic state. It is important to note that reference to the "pan-Indian" movement as employed in this study does not necessarily mean a cognitive, coordinated social movement, nor, as will be seen, that various pan-Indian issues share the support of the majority of the members of the Indian communities. Tribal identification and influence remains a strong and central focus for members of those communities.

Apparently concerted efforts, as in the case of the reburial issue, may actually be the result of an approximately simultaneous but essentially independent expression of concerns by individual tribes regarding disposition of the remains of individuals with whom affiliation is claimed. However, the individual concerns taken together, whether or not independent of one another, form an element of pan-Indian identity as effectively as if they were part of a designed national political movement. In addition, the term "activist" as used here applies to those individuals who support issues that are common to most Indian communities. It does not apply exclusively to those who are militant or who promote a pan-Indian identity.

Early postcontact Indian social movements included revitalization movements in the classic sense. In 1680 a Tewa medicine man fomented a rebellion of New Mexican Pueblo Indians against the Spanish, and in the eighteenth century a Delaware holy man led a movement rejecting Christianity and teaching a return to traditional Delaware religious beliefs. This movement was replicated in 1800 by Handsome Lake, the Seneca prophet. In 1870 the first Ghost Dance movement appeared, which predicted the ultimate removal of the white man from North America. The movement resurfaced in 1890, and other similar movements occurred after that date. The now-established Native American Church is considered by some scholars to reflect a revitalization process (Driver 1969:523–25).

The early movements were geographically and (largely) ethnically isolated. They were not pan-Indian movements of the contemporary type. In fact, there has never been a pan-Indian ethnic identity (Gill 1983:144). Newcomb (1974:233) echoes this point: "The major cultural systems of Native North America . . . encompass most of the categories of preindustrial cultures of the entire world." Hoebel gives examples of distinctly different worldviews held by the Navaho, Cheyenne, Hopi, Comanche, and Kiowa (1972:544–52; 1954:127–76). Greenberg et al. (1986:477–80) identify three basic aboriginal language stocks in North America and suggest that three different migrations into the New World took place. They divide the three stocks into eleven subgroups and nineteen hundred discrete dialects, providing evidence of a wealth of mutually unintelligible languages among precontact Indians.

In a study more directly related to our concerns, Driver (1969:373–77) describes Indian mortuary practices that run the gamut from cremation to inhumation to exposure of the corpse in trees or on special scaffolding. Robinson and Sprague (1965:442–53) describe rapid changes in mortuary practice and even variation within the same culture at the same site. Despite this pronounced diversity, efforts persist to establish a pan-Indian identity.

The character of Indian revitalization movements began to change in the nineteenth century. Kroeber (1948:439) noted that beginning with the Second Ghost Dance, around 1890, Indian revivalist movements began to diverge from prior classic revitalization patterns. The later movements cut across tribal boundaries and spread much more rapidly than previous ones. Kroeber attributed this to the employment of English as an Indian lingua franca, transportation by railroads, and enforced contact between different tribes through compulsory reservation settlements. Revitalization movements accelerated in the twentieth century, given impetus by new developments, including mass communications, urbanization, and education (Hertzberg 1973:160). Approximately 25,000 Indians served in the military during World War II, and another 50,000 were drawn to industry in new capacities, with new training and a new political agenda (Driver 1969:495). The National Congress of American Indians was formed by veterans in 1944 to advance Indian political interests (Wax 1971:145).

In 1946 Congress established the Claims Commission, enabling Indian tribes to seek restitution for lands taken from them by whites. Before the deadline for filing expired, 852 claims had been filed for twice as much acreage as exists in the continental United States. The hearings continued for at least two decades (with the assistance of fifty anthropologists) and had the important effect of educating Indians to the advantages and mechanics of legal representation (Driver 1969:495–97). These are all processes of enculturation and not isolation or revitalization, and they are directly relevant to the shape of the contemporary Indian social movement.

The single event commonly cited as marking the origin of the modern Indian movement is the American Indian Chicago Conference of 1961 coordinated by Sol Tax of the University of Chicago (Driver 1969:500–501; Lurie 1971b:462). This meeting brought together the largest intertribal common effort ever assembled, over five hundred individuals representing ninety tribes and bands. But advances in technology, cultural diversity, and increasing enculturation produced other stresses on pan-Indian identity.

Advances in communication technology, while permitting rapid dissemination of information among Indian activists, may conflict with one cultural tradition suggested as legitimately pan-Indian: consensus (not just majority vote) on strongly contended issues (Lurie 1971b:444). Although mass media contribute to the awareness of problems, directed attitudinal changes require interpersonal communication (Rogers 1971: 13). Furthermore, activists and tribal leaders may be able to reach consensus on certain issues, but the rate of the new communication does not allow sufficient time for consensus to be reached by the greater Indian constituency, especially an already diverse population that has not resolved a distinct ethnic identity.

Indeed, the possibility that the mass media may expand the context of the dialogue in Indian communities poses significant questions. For instance, do members of the Indian community become so quickly informed on issues through impersonal channels (and thus quickly form private opinions) that opportunity is denied activists and leaders to influence the formation of opinion through interpersonal communication? If so, the problem of not having the consensus so valued by the greater Indian community would be exacerbated, and additional pressure would appear to be placed on pan-Indian activists to quickly establish a pan-Indian identity in order to avoid progressive fragmentation of the Indian movement. Lurie (1971b:420) observes that the very fact that Indians of different tribal backgrounds are forced to communicate in English among themselves accelerates the impact of communication and the rate of enculturation, as the traditional Indian languages are perceived as less useful.

Attempts to bring together a diverse population under the umbrella of a single identity can be expected to inspire the invention of "traditions" with which the constituent groups can identify (Hobsbawm 1985:280–81, 307). Such invention is more likely to occur when the group in question is in a state of transition or imbalance, and it often takes the form of new or modified religious practices that are likely to be ambiguous. Pan-Indian religious beliefs are ambiguous, and because of historical variation in religion and the element of enculturation by a large segment of the Indian population, these beliefs are sometimes in conflict with those held by various factions within the Indian community. One can anticipate an inclination toward fragmentation of pan-Indian identity followed by efforts to reassert that identity. Such efforts may include the invention of a pan-Indian religious concept. Newly developed pan-Indian definitions of sacredness have emerged (Zimmerman 1985a:1), reinforced through law in the context of reburial and repatriation of prehistoric Indian remains and grave goods, which in turn serves to augment a sense of pan-Indian identity.

The extensive enculturation of the Indian population and intense exposure to the power of the legal process through the lengthy and contentious Claims Commission hearings results in aboriginal activists' methods—including recourse in court—perceived by the host culture as legitimate. The pan-Indian social movement relies heavily on law as a device for achieving its objectives. The movement has its own lawyers, such as those employed by the Native American Rights Fund, its own lobbyists in the form of the National Congress of American Indians, and its own journalists.

As might have been predicted, assertion of tribal identity and factionalization among various Indian cultures is reported to have increased since the 1970s (Lurie 1986:48, 51) and to have accelerated in the 1980s, though this latter development is attributed to factors in addition to those described above. Olson and Wilson (1984:210–13) discuss continuing assimilation of Indians into European-American society and the increasing ratio of "mixed-blood" Indians to "full-bloods" as additional factors lending momentum to accelerated factionalization of the Indian community.

Lurie (1971a:194–95) considers the current pan-Indian movement sufficiently distinct as to constitute a cultural transformation process distinguishable from classic revitalization. She calls the process a "renascence" and characterizes it as having diffuse leadership, emphasis and action that varies from place to place, and a seemingly contradictory desire for Indian identity joined with a vocal insistence on the right of separate Indian groups to persist as distinct entities.

The nature of a pan-Indian identity produces additional legal issues tangential to reburial and repatriation. These are discussed in greater detail in the specific discussion of the law, but it is relevant here to note several areas of impact. The first of these relates to standing. The courts require parties who initiate claims at court to have a direct and substantial interest in the outcome of the action, and that interest must be of a nature that the courts recognize as deserving of protection. This interest is known as standing and is required to ensure that the court is fully informed of all aspects of the facts at hand in order to make a fully informed decision.

Without the required standing, parties will not be allowed to present claims at court. A pan-Indian perspective alleges familial and spiritual identity with all prehistoric Indians and a direct interest in the disposition of their remains and grave goods. The courts generally do not recognize this as sufficient interest to establish standing at court (Rosen 1980:8–9; *A.I.A.D. v AmRep* [Dist. Ct. N. Mex. 1986]). In one New York case

(*Bailey v Miller* 1955), the court held that an Indian who was neither a descendant of the aboriginal individual whose burial was in question nor an authorized representative of a tribe affiliated with the remains had no standing to prevent disinterment of the remains. Activists have pressed for relaxation of the standard in cases involving prehistoric Indian remains and grave goods to enable a larger population of Indians to bring actions than merely those who can establish direct familial or tribal relationship with the remains.

In addition to the question of standing, central to many of these cases is the burden of proof. Aboriginal remains and artifacts have been acquired by institutions over a long and clouded period of time and sometimes under circumstances that would not survive the test of contemporary standards of acquisition (Preston 1989). Details surrounding the means of acquisition are often obscure, and museums control most such information regarding items in their respective collections. Aboriginal representatives argue that because some of the materials probably were obtained by theft from aboriginal owners and graves, there should be a presumption at law that aboriginal claimants are entitled to repatriation of aboriginal human material and associated grave goods (Echo-Hawk 1986:441). The institutions would then accept the burden of proving that they had properly obtained and maintained legal title to the material in their collections. This is counter to the usual rule at law that the plaintiff has the initial burden of establishing the merit of its claim.

With regard to museums, this placement of the burden of proof may also be in conflict with rules of customary international law. Principles of international law are often, albeit cautiously, applied when considering relationships between Indians and "mainstream" American society (Cohen 1942:39–40). Customary international law may be relevant in the context of aboriginal demands on museums for repatriation of items of aboriginal origin. If so, it has been argued that these principles place an *extra* burden on claimants to museum collections. According to Merryman (1986:100–109), these collections are considered to constitute the cultural patrimony of all humanity, not merely that of specific groups who claim interest in parts of a collection. Merryman describes the tests that are employed when international requests are made for repatriation of materials held by a museum. The tests have not previously been applied to human skeletal materials, but the arguments are analogous, and similar arguments have been raised for aboriginal remains and artifacts (Thompson 1986:3–4). In any event, the tests certainly apply to associated grave goods.

First among these tests is the general principle of repose—an existing situation should continue unless some reason is given for changing it. If a significant reason is given for change in custody and legal title to the material is uncertain, then three other tests apply:

1. Who is best able and most likely to preserve the material for the benefit of future generations? At least in the case of human material, this must be the museum because the aboriginal intent is generally to effect funerary disposition of the material.

2. Who is best able and most likely to maintain the integrity of the material? That is, who can best put the material in its original context for the benefit of understanding the material and its function? This test might best be passed by the aboriginal community related to the material if its intent is to preserve and maintain the material. Seemingly, this would especially be true in the case of sacred artifacts.

3. Who will best hold the common cultural heritage available to humanity in general for study and education? Again, with appropriate limitations and safeguards, this might be passed by both the aboriginal and museum communities. The thrust of customary international law is for preservation and study of the cultural patrimony of humanity for the ultimate benefit of all.

Whether a claimant will pass these tests depends in large part on the intent of that claimant toward ultimate disposition of the materials in question. The tests applied by international law express a number of values: a high regard for the respectful treatment of remains, a sense of panhuman identity, a bias against private control of cultural heritage, an emphasis on preservation of objects of antiquity, and an endorsement for the advancement of knowledge and understanding.

The element of factionalism also creates problems at law. As seen, the Indian activists do not always enjoy a constituency among the general Indian population. If an institution is forced or is willing to offer remains or grave goods to an Indian community for appropriate disposition, to whom should the institution tender the items? Roderick Sprague describes separate factions among the Sahaptin-speaking Indians of the northwest United States who have differing views on the appropriate disposition of items from the graves of direct ancestors (Quick 1985:51). Institutional administrators may suffer censure and possible legal liability for transferring items from their institutions' collections to individuals who are not recognized by the relevant Indian community. A persistent question in this issue is, Who speaks for the Indians? (Adams 1989b:5; Thompson 1986:2–3).

The pan-Indian movement seeks to promote a unified sense of Indian identity. It values traditional histories. These traditional and usually oral histories tend to obscure Indian cultural variation. On the other hand, archaeology, museum collections, and studies in physical anthropology tend to demonstrate cultural variation among prehistoric Indian populations. Anthropology has been characterized by some Indian activists as racist and fundamentally biased, and thus injurious to aboriginal interests and obscuring an objective appreciation of aboriginal life and values (Deloria 1973, 1974). At least among some Indian activists, archaeological and other professional efforts appear to have little utility (see, for example, Cecil Antone in Quick 1985:103).

From this perspective, the educational or scientific value of Indian material in collections is grossly subordinate to their intrinsic cultural and religious value and their significance as symbols for strengthening pan-Indian identity. In addition, there is outrage at the perceived offense to traditional religious beliefs and violation of the remains of individuals considered ancestral. Efforts to establish aboriginal recognition of a pan-Indian common cause are served by drawing together the Indian community to demand repatriation of prehistoric Indian remains and grave goods. Members of the scientific and museological community offer resistance because they do not share the objectives of the activists and therefore tend to place greater relative value on the educational and scientific utility of the items in collections.

Members of the Indian community respond by declaring Indian cultural "uniqueness" and stressing a pan-Indian worldview distinct from that held by the scientific and museological community. The concept of a worldview may be too broad to accurately explain differences in opinion, however. A worldview comprises the basic assumptions of a people about the world in which they live and their place in it (Keesing 1976: 571). It is a way of looking at reality that provides a coherent view of the world (Kearney 1984:41). One can expect that a population exposed to approximately three hundred years of enculturation would not have a worldview completely different in most respects from the larger population. In the issue at hand, the differences appear to lie with conflicts in priorities given to competing values generally shared, not to a conflict in general perceptions of reality.

The supposed disparity in worldviews usually offered is roughly that Indians believe the individual human spirit maintains a relationship with its earthly remains until those remains totally decompose, and that European-American professionals, on the other hand, view the remains as inanimate objects for study with little regard for the human beings that the remains represent. As pointed out earlier, this ostensible Indian belief does not appear to be universal among Indians, just as the position claimed for the professionals does not apply for all. One consistent pan-Indian plea, however, is for respectful treatment of the remains.

The professional community protests that it also values the respectful treatment of human remains. However, the occasional incidence of public display of prehistoric Indian remains and sometimes insensitive curation practices belie the alleged respect by some professionals for the objects with which they deal. The sometimes casual curation of the mingled remains of various individuals in cardboard boxes and sacks does not suggest reverence for the contents.

But the real issue appears to be the relative ordering of the specific values that lead to a definition of respect and whether mortuary disposition of the remains is to be given priority over other values, such as those pertaining to education, advancement of knowledge, and the ownership of private property. In this regard, the Indian community has little basis from which to complain of a difference in worldview from that held by the mainstream European-American community. Indeed, the Indian activists' success in promoting and achieving remedial legislation at the state and national levels may be seen as a result of a perception by mainstream legislators of a shared value between the Indian groups and the greater American constituency regarding the respectful disposition of all human remains, including those of prehistoric Indians.

Whether that shared general value will be maintained when the new laws are recognized as conflicting with other values has yet to be determined. Some of those other values are also protected at law, and the conflict of competing values has already resulted in legal actions pertaining to the separation of church and state, the right to pursue a profession without undue interference on the part of the state, and prohibition of the state from taking private property without just compensation. These issues are discussed in greater detail later.

Given increasing factionalization of Indian communities, barriers at law to pan-Indian identity, and increasing enculturation of the Indian community, why does even an amorphous sense of pan-Indian identity persist? Walker (1972:744–46) views pan-Indian identity as a response to, and a mode of, acculturation. It is a vehicle to allow the individual Indian to interact with the larger host culture, and it is a mechanism by which distinct Indian cultural groups can interact with one another. Are there, in fact, consistent and distinct pan-Indian cultural characteristics? Lurie (1971b:444–48) and Olson and Wilson (1984:213–19) describe several pan-Indian cultural elements that distinguish Indian attitudes and values from those held by European Americans. Among other factors, these include emphasis on decision by consensus, emphasis on oratory and humor, institutionalized sharing with disapproval of greed and self-ishness, mistrust of overt expressions of ambition, tolerance of personal idiosyncracies, and physical withdrawal from stressful personal situations.

Lurie (1971b:448) points out that the very presence of European Americans affords a contrast that serves to make evident to Indians similarities among themselves that previously they had accepted as normal human behavior. Moreland (1989) states that whatever the variation among Indian groups, they consider themselves more like one another than they are to European Americans. Gill (1983:144–45) describes the phenomenon of pan-Indian identity as a reaction to European-American pressure on tribal traditions and identities, and Wax (1971:155) believes there is a growing fission between political and cultural pan-Indian identification. Those who are interested in developing a pan-Indian cultural identity in the arts do not necessarily have the same goals as those who aspire to pan-Indian political positions, although the latter claim to represent the former.

Finally, Wilson and Zingg (1974:416) comment that other American minorities have independent sources of security and ethnic identity—Asia, Africa, Latin America, or areas of Polynesia, for instance. American Indians can look only to themselves for their sense of identity. Despite the growing Indian factionalization and other complexities surrounding the pan-Indian phenomenon, there does appear to be a fundamental, though vague, pan-Indian sense of community vis-à-vis the European-American community.

However complex the underlying mechanisms, a sense of pan-Indian community persists and has taken on an international scope, as indigenous aboriginal populations in areas colonized by foreign powers now look to the American aboriginal experience as a model. The Indian model has been suggested as a predictive tool for assessing future experience in Asia, Australia, and Africa (Walker 1972:745). (In fact, the Australian aboriginal campaign for compulsory interment of prehistoric remains and grave goods may be progressing faster and in a more extreme direction than the comparable movement in the United States [Lewin 1984:393–94; Ubelaker and Grant 1989:279–80].) Pan-Indian representatives have traveled abroad to assess similar situations in other countries and to discuss the matter with aboriginal representatives there (Quick 1988:3). Advances in transportation and communication technology undoubtedly aid in the growing global aborigine information network. As with the pan-Indian movement, the full effect on the international movement of new technologies remains to be determined.

Developments in the United States are reported to have contributed to aboriginal confrontations in Australia and Canada (Sutton 1985:5; Bates 1989:4–5). Underscoring the extent of the international aboriginal network, in August 1989 the World Archaeological Congress—in association with the International Indian Treaty Council, the World Council of Indigenous Peoples, and American Indians Against Desecration—held a special intercongress entitled "Archaeological Ethics and the Treatment of the Dead." The purpose was to establish an international forum for the exchange of opinions and experiences and for the development of strategies addressing the issue of appropriate disposition of prehistoric aboriginal remains and grave goods.

Not simply a domestic phenomenon, the pan-Indian movement in the United States may be part of an international social dynamic centered around revitalization movements of native populations in areas colonized by outside powers. If the present pan-Indian process is moving toward a larger pan-aboriginal global dynamic with shared networks and interests, no doubt new values and strategies, as well as new and instructive issues at law, will surface.

3 General and Federal Law

Law is a cultural ordering of relationships among individuals (Hoebel 1954:47–51), reflecting modal values held by members of a group. As situations change, that is, as new values are introduced, the consequences at law change. "What is the law?" is a difficult question to answer until all the possible relevant variables are considered. Even then, if significant competing values exist, or if the law is new and its application to certain values has not been resolved, the answer may be elusive. If strong emotional and intellectual appeal is made to a specific narrow modal value held by the population (for example, respectful treatment of human remains)—one previously dormant until awakened to cognitive consideration through consciousness-raising techniques employed by activists—the consequence at law may be ambiguous.

Consciousness-raising techniques to awaken dormant values include employment of the mass media, raising dramatic cases at law (even when the case is expected to be lost), and intensive lobbying. These techniques can produce awareness of the problems caused by the interplay of conflicting value systems (Frizzell 1974:341), but they may also obscure consideration of other competing values that conflict with the cause being promoted. Thus, although specific legislation may be enacted to satisfy concerns regarding newly considered values, the longevity and the application in practice of those new statutes may be in question until the institutions of law (in the present context, the courts, the administrative and enforcement institutions, and the legislatures) have resolved the ordering of competing cultural values to the modal satisfaction of the citizenry.

In the case of the law in the United States pertaining to the disposition of prehistoric aboriginal remains and grave goods, many variables must be considered. Each variable reflects the impact of different cultural values on the result at law. One variable is the nature of the item. When it is human material, the degree of antiquity and identity of ethnicity are important, as are questions pertaining to the conditions of interment:

Was it an intentional burial, and, if so, was it part of a cemetery and was the cemetery abandoned? If the item is what commonly is referred to as an artifact, questions of association with human burials are raised. Even if there is no funerary association, the degree of "sacredness" of the object may be important.

Another important factor is where the item was found. Different consequences at law depend on whether the object was on federal, state, tribal, local-municipality, or private land. And the law will vary from state to state, from reservation to reservation, and from municipality to municipality. Who has current possession of the object? Is it in the possession of a private individual, a state or federal employee or institution, or a museum? If a museum, is it private, state, or federal?

How the possessor came to possess the object also constitutes a significant factor. Did a transfer occur? Did the transferor give title or mere custody? Did the transferor have good title to the object or was he a thief? What precautions did the transferee take to ensure proper title? Who is making the claim for an interest in the object superior to that of the party in possession? And what is the nature of the interest claimed? All of these questions and more may affect the answer at law.

Common Law and General Statutory Law

In the United States' system of jurisprudence, formal law may arise by the will and act of the legislature, statutory law, or it may arise through a cumulative body of case law resolved through judicial decisions, common law. Generally, common law and statutory law pertaining to cemeteries and burials are within the province of the individual states. However, the states borrow from one another both common-law principles and statutory models. These laws can be addressed on general and historical levels to achieve a perspective on the development of general national law.

American common law is derived from the common law of England, although it frequently departs from that base. Each state enjoys its own body of common law through a historical accretion of decisions rendered by its own courts and the selective adoption of decisions from other jurisdictions. In considering the legal ramifications of the proper disposition of prehistoric human remains and grave goods, common law is of interest. English common law did not consider bodies as property. Neither heirs nor anyone else could sue at law for injury to, or disturbance of, a dead body (Schneider 1989:1). Disturbing burials is another matter. England still does not accept the principle of separation of church and state, a concept carefully protected in the United States. Under the English system, burials were to be in churchyards. Thus, the parson sued in the English ecclesiastical courts for disturbance of the soil of the grave site. But even remains located within church confines were often treated in a careless and haphazard manner (McGuire 1989:172–73). Those unfortunates who were interred outside the confines of the churchyard were afforded no protection against confiscation and use of their remains. Hubert (1989:136) reports that bodies of decedents whose relatives and friends were too poor to bury them securely were freely dug up and sold by the thousands.

The experience in the United States is different. There has never been an ecclesiastical court in this country, and there are many burials unconnected with any church. Accordingly, American law has tended to find solutions to issues of conflicting values (for example, respectful treatment of human remains versus integrity of ownership of private property) more responsive to the American context. Thus, definitions of cemeteries replaced church burial yards with formally dedicated property, and definitions of burials referred to formally marked inhumations in place of those contained in church cemeteries. A substitute also had to be found for the parson as the party entitled to bring action for the desecration of graves. This need was satisfied by new principles of standing and by a declaration that desecration of formal cemeteries and burials constituted a crime against the state and was therefore punishable through police authority.

Historical accident plays an important role in the formation of law. Common law is a body of legal principles developed over time through the consideration by the courts of a sequence of factual experiences involving competing values. Common law and burial statutes specific to the American setting began to be formed in the eighteenth century. A strong foundation for American common law had developed by the end of the nineteenth century, all based on experiences involving the exigencies of life in the United States as experienced by the legislators and as presented in the court room.

When the foundations of this nation's common law were being formed, the courts and legislators had little opportunity to consider issues involving disposition of prehistoric aboriginal remains and grave goods. One reason was the lack of excavation of Indian burial sites. Professionals at the time, with some exceptions, believed that Indians had only recently arrived in the Americas (therefore lacking archaeological depth), that they were basically nomadic (and similarly without archaeological remains of interest), and that they were too simple to have built the numerous burial, effigy, and temple mounds. Rather, these structures were variously attributed to survivors of Mu or Atlantis, or to wandering Scandinavians or the lost tribes of Israel. Such attitudes helped justify European-American confiscation of Indian lands and, coincidentally, delayed the adoption in the United States of European technical innovations (such as stratigraphy) for archaeological excavation of sites with significant "time depth" (Willey and Sabloff 1980:34–57; Trigger 1980).

Accordingly, there was little excavation of Indian sites by either professionals or looters, and there was little opportunity for the courts to consider issues involving disposition of prehistoric aboriginal remains and grave goods. There were aberrational incidents during the eighteenth and early nineteenth centuries, such as the request in 1868 by the surgeon general of the United States for his field officers to secure all the Indian skeletons that they were able. This resulted in the confiscation of the skeletons of several thousand individuals. However, such collection did not involve archaeological effort, and the question of its legality was not brought to court.

Indians at the time were not inclined to bring to American courts issues of their daily life. There were trials involving treaty disputes and war crimes but not problems in intratribal domestic relations, community disputes, issues of descent and distribution, or property rights. Indians had their own effective tribunals and techniques to resolve their problems without resort to mainstream courts (Hoebel 1954). Furthermore, early American courts, like politicians and archaeologists of the time, were likely to be racially biased, and Indians had little reason to have confidence in them.

At a sensitive time when American courts were developing an experience-based common law and legislators were enacting specific statutes for cemeteries and burials to account for American requirements, the courts and lawmakers were not allowed the benefit of considering practical issues related to appropriate disposition of prehistoric aboriginal remains and grave goods or regarding the property rights of Indians to these items. Thus, when issues later surfaced in the courts, the judicial system was forced to apply an established body of statutes and common law to situations that law had not previously considered and with which it was ill suited to deal. This resulted in decisions like *Carter v City of Zanesville* (Ohio, 1898), in which the court held that decomposed skeletal remains of prehistoric Indians did not constitute a body as contemplated at law, and *Wana the Bear v Community Construction, Inc.* (California, 1982), in which an established Miwok traditional cemetery was held to not constitute a cemetery for purposes of the California state statute.

The American emphasis on the concept of private property has compounded the problem. The integrity of private ownership of real property is an important value in the American ethos and is reflected in the United States Constitution under the Fifth and Fourteenth Amendments. Generally, American property law grants to the landowner ownership of all objects embedded in the land. Lacking common law to the contrary, this applies to Indian burials and to all owners, whether private or governmental (Moore 1987:5). However, concern for respectful treatment of human remains is also a strongly held American value, and in response common law has produced a variety of theories by which this value is sometimes maintained.

Some jurisdictions grant a quasi-property right in the remains to various categories of individuals related to the deceased (Bowman 1989: 167–68). These interests may be characterized by labels at law other than a property right in the remains, such as easement or license to intrude on the land in which the remains are interred. In the most liberal jurisdictions, individuals allowed to maintain a legal action to protect remains may be friends or relatives of the deceased. A moderate view allows action by the next of kin, and the strictest position allows only the direct heirs to bring an action (Schneider 1989:2–3). These three levels result from the degree of interest in the matter that establishes the standing of the plaintiffs necessary for the court to hear the action. Plaintiffs with standing are then allowed to protect the remains and to direct the proper disposition of them. It is difficult for living Indians to prove direct familial descent from prehistoric aboriginal remains sufficient to constitute the standing required to maintain an action at law to protect the remains (Rosen 1980:6).

One Louisiana case (*Charrier v Bell*) is often cited as representing a new trend allowing greater freedom of standing for aborigines to claim buried grave goods (see Bowman 1989:172; Echo-Hawk 1986:447–48, 1988: 2–3; Moore 1987:5–6). This case is a weak reed on which to rest hopes of liberalized standing. Charrier removed Indian materials from land without the permission or knowledge of the property owners. The state of Louisiana purchased the property and formally subordinated its claim to the grave goods to the Tunica-Biloxi tribe, whose ancestors had originally deposited them. Confused reasoning by the court mingles principles of title to the goods and to the underlying land (Bowman

1989:172–74). And the decision is specifically based on the Napoleonic Code of France. Although this does not necessarily mean that the results would have been different in other states, it does mean that courts in other jurisdictions are less likely to consider the case as ready precedent.

Cemeteries and burials are given special protection at law. Generally, this imposes on the property owner an obligation to avoid desecration and disturbance of the graves. However, cemeteries and burials may be abandoned, and abandonment removes these obligations from the land-owner. The definition of abandonment varies among different jurisdictions. In general, when the identity of the decedents is lost, the grounds are not maintained as a cemetery, no further burials are made, and the remains have decomposed, the cemetery will be considered abandoned (see *Carter v City of Zanesville* [Ohio, 1898]). Similarly, decomposed skeletal remains have been held to not fall within the definition of corpse or body for purposes of the Ohio grave-robbing statutes (*State v Glass*, 1971).

Clearly, common-law treatment of bodies, cemeteries, and burials does not afford much protection to prehistoric human remains. For example, in the California case of *Wana the Bear v Community Construction, Inc.*, the city of Stockton was permitted to bulldoze through a known cemetery of the Miwok Indians, abandoned by the Indians because of American military action, and thus destroy the graves of over two hundred Miwok individuals. The California state legislature responded by enacting specific legislation protecting aboriginal remains. When the common law or the existing statutory regime fails to preserve contemporary modal values, recourse is sought through legislation, either new and specific legislation or the extended application of existing legislation. When the law does not provide equal protection to all citizens in regard to a particular matter, issues under the U.S. Constitution may be involved, as discussed below.

Federal Legislation

Legislation takes precedence over common law. The federal government has enacted a historical sequence of statutes that reflect intensifying values regarding the protection of prehistoric aboriginal remains and an increasing awareness of problems related to that protection. The laws apply to federal land, Indian reservations, and in some cases to state property where federal funds or security are used to develop that property. The focus of these laws is to preserve and protect cultural heritage sites and objects located within them against loss (Wilson and Zingg 1974:414). This is a significant point, since this purpose conflicts with the objective of some Indian groups to recover and reinter or otherwise dispose of prehistoric aboriginal remains and grave goods. These statutes are considered below in chronological order.

The Antiquities Act of 1906

The Antiquities Act was passed shortly after the second Ghost Dance of the 1890s while memory of the Indian revitalization movement was relatively recent. The act was first proposed in 1900 but became embroiled in a six-year battle between politicians who then controlled the archaeological resources and the professional organizations (e.g., the Archaeological Institute of America and the American Association for the Advancement of Science) that promoted the legislation to protect the resources (King et al. 1977:18–20).

That portion of the act relevant to this study gave exclusive jurisdiction and control to the federal government of all prehistoric resources located on property owned or controlled by the federal government. Properly qualified institutions are granted permits for excavation undertaken for the benefit of reputable museums for permanent preservation in those museums of items recovered. There is no provision regarding consideration of aboriginal interests in any objects recovered (Echo-Hawk 1985:11–12).

In practice, the Smithsonian Institution reviews and makes recommendations on all Antiquity Act permit applications. If a museum should cease to be able to continue preservation of items recovered under permit, the collections are transferred to the Smithsonian for curation in the national depository, thus emphasizing a value preference for preservation and study of the objects rather than for repatriation and reinterment, or other funerary disposition.

The Antiquities Act has not been repealed, but it has little current impact. The act contains provisions imposing criminal penalties on those who violate its strictures. In 1974 the provisions were declared unconstitutionally vague (*United States v Diaz*, 9th Cir. 1974). The court held that penalties imposed for removal or destruction of "objects of antiquity" did not allow individuals to know in advance of their acts precisely what constituted "antiquity." The ambit of the Antiquities Act is now largely covered by the Archaeological Resources Protection Act of 1979.

Historic Sites Act of 1935

Although this act has little relevance to the problem of disposition of prehistoric aboriginal remains and grave goods, it indicates the continuing national concern for preservation of antiquities. The act was part of President Roosevelt's New Deal and for the first time asserted a broad federal concern for the nation's historic properties (King et al. 1977:23).

The National Park Service is authorized to conduct programs to locate, record, preserve, mark, and commemorate properties of national significance. The act establishes an Advisory Board on National Parks, Historical Sites, Buildings, and Monuments. Up to eleven citizens are appointed by the secretary of the Department of the Interior to sit on the board, and preference is given to those with academic expertise rather than to those of aboriginal origin (Wilson and Zingg 1974:426). The National Park Service exists under the umbrella of the Department of the Interior, and the act underscores the central role of that department in federal preservation. The resource survey conducted under the act was a precursor to the current National Register of Historic Places (Perry 1985:6–7).

The Reservoir Salvage Act of 1960

This act supplements the Historic Sites Act. Essentially, it provides a procedure to avoid loss of historical and archaeological data that might otherwise occur through construction of dams by federal agencies or licensees (Wilson and Zingg 1974:427). It allows the secretary of the Department of the Interior to make archaeological surveys of areas to be affected by the construction of dams. However, the secretary is authorized to preserve only sites of exceptional significance, and then the preservation activity must be conducted as expeditiously as possible.

The National Historic Preservation Act of 1966

This act (NHPA) authorizes the interior secretary to maintain a national register of districts, sites, buildings, structures, and objects significant to American history, architecture, archaeology, and culture, thereby expanding greatly the register mandated under the Historic Sites Act of 1935. Entries can include some Indian burial grounds and graves (Wilson and Zingg 1974:429–30). The NHPA also establishes the twenty-member Advisory Council on Historic Preservation.

The NHPA requires federal agencies to "establish a program to locate, inventory, and nominate to the secretary all properties under the agency's ownership or control" that appear to qualify for registration on the National Register of Historic Places (16 U.S.C. Sect. 470h-2[a][2]). Once a property is so listed or declared eligible for registration, then the Advisory Council on Historic Preservation may comment on any federal action that might adversely affect such property. Federal agencies, however, are not required to follow the advice of the advisory council.

Designed to protect property from destruction, the NHPA evidences a continued priority in the 1960s of modal values for curation of prehistoric items. It was not designed to repatriate remains or grave goods to aborigine claimants. Further, it is procedural and not substantive. For items registered, the NHPA ensures that all perspectives and values can be publicly heard before federal action is taken that might adversely affect those items. Administrators of federal projects must publicly justify in advance plans that threaten registered prehistoric property. Accordingly, though criteria for registration are stringent, aboriginal groups might press for inclusion on the National Register of Historic Places those structures and sites considered important to their cultural identity.

The Department of Transportation Act of 1966

This act created the Department of Transportation. Of relevance here is its requirement that the department consider the impact of proposed highway or other transportation projects on historic sites of federal, state, or local significance. The department cannot use land from such sites unless there is no feasible and prudent alternative, and steps are taken to ensure the adequate recovery of archaeological materials.

Although the act is broader than the NHPA in that it considers sites other than those registered on the National Register, it applies only to the Department of Transportation and not to any other federal department or agency. It also evidences a continuing emphasis on preservation, not repatriation of remains and property to aborigines, and it gives priority to values of economic development.

The Administrative Procedures Act of 1966

This act is important because it gives citizens standing to demand judicial review of administrative proceedings conducted under the other legislation discussed. However, the issue of standing remains a significant barrier to aborigines. The plaintiff must suffer legal wrong or be affected adversely or be aggrieved as a result of federal agency action, and the injury suffered must be of a nature recognized by the court as entitled to judicial consideration. The connection of an individual aborigine to an incident threatening alleged pan-aboriginal cultural values is tenuous at law and unlikely to qualify as standing (Wilson and Zingg 1974:441). One case (*A.I.A.D., et al., v AMREP Southwest, Inc.*, D. N.M. 1986) held that Indian interest groups have no standing to bring action unless their members have standing to sue in their own right as individuals, the interests injured are germane to the group's purpose, and neither the claim asserted nor the relief requested requires the participation of individual members in the lawsuit.

The National Environmental Policy Act of 1969

Under this act (NEPA), federal agencies are required to file environmental impact statements (EIS) concerning the impact on the physical and cultural environment of federally assisted projects. The agencies are required to use an interdisciplinary approach, including systematic use of the social sciences. Public hearings and opportunity for comment on an EIS are required, and this opportunity to comment is as available to American aborigines as it is to all other citizens (Rosen 1980:13).

Again the focus is on preservation and not on repatriation of prehistoric objects. However, NEPA has been employed by Indians to preserve sites that are significant to them. In 1972 a federal district court sustained an injunction against a federal highway project threatening an Indian lookout (*Indian Lookout Alliance v Volpe*, S.D. Iowa, 1972). Relative anonymity of the site has suggested to some that NEPA might be applied to protect essentially Indian values and institutions (Wilson and

Zingg 1974:435). If this interpretation is accurate, the decision is one of the first at law, in the context of preservation, to suggest a trend toward European-American implementation of a value of consideration of contemporary Indian cultural sensitivities.

The provisions of NEPA remain procedural, but significant weight is given to historic preservation in balancing the value and methods of a proposed project against threats to the natural and cultural environment. And the procedure is stringent. The sponsoring federal agency must provide a written report addressing concerns raised and describing the nature of its account of and response to the factors in controversy.

Surface Mining Control and Reclamation Act of 1977

This act gives the interior secretary authority to issue permits for mining on federal property. In the exercise of this authority, the secretary is required to consider the effect of the proposed mining on the environment. Permits may be denied if the activity would result in significant injury to important historic, cultural, or scientific properties (Bowman 1989:195). Again, reference to preservation of cultural values surfaces in the formal law.

American Indian Religious Freedom Act of 1978

This act (AIRFA) is yet another procedural statute, but it is one that specifically considers Indian cultural values, continuing the trend at formal law to protect recognition of contemporary aboriginal cultural values. AIRFA stresses the rights of Indians to freedom of religion protected by the First Amendment to the U.S. Constitution. Although there is comment suggesting that AIRFA may grant substantive rights to Indians, several court decisions, and especially those involving land cases, indicate that it is merely procedural (O'Brien 1988:iii–viii). This is the prevailing interpretation (Bowman 1989:191; Echo-Hawk 1986:452). A recent Supreme Court case (*Lyng v Northwest Indian Cemetery Protective Ass'n*, S.Ct. 1988) held that although Indian religious beliefs may be sincere and proposed governmental action would affect them adversely, unless the government action was designed to prevent the Indians' practice of their religion, the Indians had no right under the First Amendment to the U.S. Constitution to prevent the government action.

Under AIRFA, federal agencies must consider the effect of their projects on Indian religious beliefs, objects, and practices. Just as with other procedural statutes, however, the agencies are not required to do more than consider the impact. They are not required to protect Indian cultural and religious beliefs or to mitigate damage to them. But Indians are provided a forum in which to publicly present both their cultural values and the basis for their objections to federal projects that affect them. Among other purposes, this forum can be used as a consciousness-raising device to increase mainstream American awareness of Indian cultural sensitivities.

Archaeological Resources Protection Act of 1979

This act (ARPA) is the operative legislation that effectively replaces the Antiquities Act of 1906. ARPA introduces the concept of "archaeological resource," defined as any material remains of past human life or activities that is at least one hundred years old. Thus, the ambiguity of the Antiquities Act is cured. Human physical remains are specifically included within the definition of archaeological resource.

ARPA specifically requires the consideration of AIRFA in the promulgation of its rules, but again only consideration is required. In addition, Indians must be given notice of permits for excavation on non-Indian public land that might result in harm to Indian religious or cultural sites. However, any Indian complaints are advisory only and need not be heeded. Permits are required for any excavation on federal or Indian lands, except that Indians may excavate without permit on tribal lands. The relevant Indian governing body has control over the terms and conditions of permits on land controlled by it. For other federal lands, the federal land manager has control over the permitting process.

The emphasis of the legislation is on preservation of archaeological resources. Objects recovered from federal land are the property of the federal government. The prevailing interpretation of ARPA is that it prevents repatriation and reburial of prehistoric aboriginal remains and grave goods because it requires recovered objects to be preserved by a suitable institution (Bowman 1989:188, 189). On the other hand, archaeological resources recovered from Indian land are the property of the tribe.

Penalties for violations of ARPA are much severer than penalties under the Antiquities Act. Penalties include initial fines of up to $10,000 and imprisonment for up to one year. But if the cost of restoration plus the value of the archaeological resource taken or damaged totals more than $5,000, the amount of the possible fine may be up to $20,000 with imprisonment for up to two years. Further violations incur fines of up to $100,000 and imprisonment for up to five years. Once more, these are measures designed to encourage preservation and not to promote repatriation of aboriginal cultural patrimony.

National Museum of the American Indian Act of 1989

This act continues the trend toward increasing federally legislated recognition of aboriginal concerns in this issue. The law establishes, within the Smithsonian Institution, the National Museum of the American Indian. Among other charges, the museum is authorized to receive the important aboriginal collections of the Heye Foundation of New York. The collections are to be placed in a new facility to be constructed on the Mall in Washington, D.C. The new museum is governed by a board of trustees comprised of the secretary of the Smithsonian, one assistant secretary, and twenty-three other members, of whom at least twelve must be Indian. The museum is established for the benefit of the general public, but priority is given to Indian interests. In the loan of collections, participation in exhibits, and rendering of technical advice, preference must be given by the museum to requests of Indian groups. The act gives very high priority to the inventory of Indian remains and grave goods held in Smithsonian collections.

Indian tribes may request repatriation of human remains and associated grave goods affiliated with the requesting tribe. Affiliation is to be established or denied by a preponderance of the available evidence. To assist in the repatriation process, the secretary of the interior is authorized to issue financial grants to interested Indian groups. In general, similar privileges are extended to native Hawaiian groups, although the authority to issue facilitating grants to native Hawaiian claimants has not been included in the act.

Native American Grave Protection and Repatriation Act of 1990

This act was signed by President George Bush on November 16, 1990, and is the strongest current federal legislation recognizing the interests of contemporary aboriginal communities in prehistoric aboriginal remains and artifacts. The new law has two basic foci. First, it applies to human remains and certain artifacts discovered after the effective date of the act. Second, it addresses collections of aboriginal materials held by federal agencies and museums receiving federal support. The act specifically exempts the Smithsonian Institution from its application, and it does not apply to materials found on private or state property.

Native American cultural items and remains excavated or discovered on federal or tribal lands are placed under the ownership or control of native American groups in stated order of priority. In the case of human remains and grave goods, ownership lies with the lineal descendants. If lineal descendants cannot be established or if sacred objects, objects of cultural patrimony, or funerary objects unassociated with human remains are in question, ownership vests in the Indian tribe or native Hawaiian group on whose land the items were found. Otherwise, it is next vested in the group with closest cultural affiliation. Finally, failing all of the above, ownership is in the group recognized as aboriginally occupying the area in which the objects are discovered.

Scientific and salvage excavations are permitted under cover of a permit under ARPA. If on federal land, there must be consultation with the relevant native American group. If on tribal land, the consent of the relevant aboriginal group must be obtained.

In the event of inadvertent discovery (such as through construction, logging, mining, and agriculture) of native American remains and grave goods, written notice of such discovery must be given to the federal agency with primary management responsibility over the area, or if found on tribal lands, to the aboriginal organization. All activity in the area must cease immediately and the items discovered must be reasonably protected. Activity may not resume until thirty days following certification by the federal agency or appropriate aboriginal group that the written notice has been properly given to them.

Each federal agency and museum receiving federal support is given five years in which to inventory native American human remains and associated grave goods in their possession or control. Extensions of time may be granted by the secretary of the interior when demonstrated efforts of good faith prove inadequate to complete the inventory in the time allowed. Within six months of completing the inventory, the museums and agencies must notify appropriate aboriginal groups. The notice must identify all items and must be accompanied by a description of the circumstances surrounding acquisition of the materials.

The inventories must also list items that cannot be culturally identified. For sacred objects, objects of cultural patrimony, and funerary objects unassociated with human remains, a summary inventory must be made in lieu of an object-by-object inventory. The summary must be completed within three years of the effective date of the act. All relevant records and documentation must be made available to aboriginal groups. Lineal descendants or appropriate groups may then require repatriation of items under generally the same priorities established for items newly discovered.

Trafficking in aboriginal human remains and cultural items obtained or held in contravention of the act is made a crime punishable by a fine and imprisonment for a term of up to one year for a first offense. Violations by museums and federal agencies incur a civil penalty to be set by the secretary of the interior.

A review committee is to be appointed by the secretary of the interior to supervise compliance with and administration of the act. Federal grants are authorized to assist aboriginal groups and museums in making use of or complying with the act. The act also recognizes the possibility and value of regional solutions to these issues. It specifically permits agencies and museums to enter into agreements with appropriate aboriginal groups, and such agreements will prevail over the provisions of this act.

Federal Policies

While not constituting formal law per se, policies implemented by federal agencies charged with enforcement of the laws have great practical effect in the operation of the law. Because a review of significant policies may also grant insight into values and value formation, some of these policies are described here.

Advisory Council on Historic Preservation

The Advisory Council is established under NHPA and charged with the responsibility of reviewing the potential impact by federal projects on properties listed or eligible to be listed in the National Register. The Advisory Council announced its policy in September 1988 in Gallup, New Mexico.

In brief, the policy states a preference for retention, *in situ*, of human remains and grave goods. Necessary disinterment should be by respectful and scientific means, with subsequent reburial. Scientific studies should be performed only under justified research projects, in accord with agreed-upon schedules and followed by reburial. If scientific studies are repugnant to descendants of the deceased, the value of the research project must be weighed against the offense to the descendants.

The policy does not define "descendant" and therefore does not appear to solve the problems of pan-Indian representatives who might wish to complain but who are not directly related to the deceased. Neither does the policy explain how reburial, which necessarily entails destruction and loss of material, can be reconciled by a statutory body whose function is to preserve objects and sites of significance. Retention in perpetuity can only occur where the property is of overwhelming scientific value, and that presumes a present scientific knowledge and prescience capable of predicting future scientific advances and requirements. Conversely, the policy does not mandate repatriation to aboriginal representatives of human remains or grave goods. But it does provide striking evidence of increasing federal recognition and consideration of aboriginal cultural sensitivities.

The Department of the Interior

The Department of the Interior (DOI) policy was written in 1982 and is notable because other agencies, especially those with limited experience in archaeological matters, tend to follow DOI guidelines when issuing permits under ARPA (Bowman 1989:159; Ubelaker and Grant 1989:273–74). These guidelines are administered by the National Park Service, a bureau of the DOI.

The guidelines provide that when human remains are encountered, the responsible agency will attempt to locate identified descendants of the deceased. Failing this, notification will be made to living groups with established affinity to the deceased. Finally, groups will be notified who may have an interest in the disposition of the remains based on generalized cultural affinity.

The agency is not required to follow the requests of any of the groups contacted. Neither is the agency prohibited by the guidelines from reburying the remains, though (as discussed below) there may be statutory prohibition against reburial. There is no provision for repatriation to aboriginal groups of remains or grave goods.

The National Park Service

In 1987 the National Park Service (NPS) published a separate "Native American Relationships Management Policy," which largely tracks DOI policy but also specifically addresses museum collections. In regard to these collections, the NPS may repatriate artifacts and specimens when it is otherwise lawful to do so and the native American representatives can demonstrate that the material is their inalienable communal property (Ubelaker and Grant 1989:273).

This latter provision does little more than recite the state of the law. If the aboriginal group can demonstrate that an object is their inalienable communal property and the NPS has no legal right to retain it, then clearly the aboriginal group is entitled to it by operation of law and not by the policy. However, the statement is important as one of the first instances at law of federal recognition that repatriation of property claimed by aboriginal groups is possible.

The U.S. Forest Service

The U.S. Forest Service (USFS), an agency of the Department of Agriculture, has adopted a broad reburial policy (Schneider et al. 1988: 1–2). The policy became effective in January 1988 for the southern and eastern regions. (Schneider and Beckes 1989:1). Reportedly, its genesis was the remarkable perception held by the USFS that "exclusive access to human remains and associated grave goods by scientists may no longer be discretionary *in the national will*" (Schneider and Beckes 1989:5; emphasis added). Thus, momentum increased for federal recognition and protection of aboriginal cultural sensitivities. USFS policy presumes that reburial of human remains and associated grave goods will occur. The policy encourages preservation, *in situ,* of remains discovered in the national forests. Consultation with interested groups is required. If the remains are of native American origin, the ambit of interested parties includes tribal governing bodies and state Indian affairs commissions (Bowman 1989:161–62). In the event that the remains must be removed, scientific study can be conducted for a period of up to one year unless the regional forester grants an extension for a longer period. Remains and grave goods presently curated must also be considered for reburial. No procedure exists for repatriation of items to aboriginal claimants.

The USFS's mandatory reburial policy reportedly raised serious objections from the DOI, which denounced it as being too restrictive and destructive of archaeological materials (Ubelaker and Grant 1989:274). In addition, the inevitable destruction through reinterment of the remains and grave goods is alleged to conflict with the provisions of ARPA. Conflict of the policy with at least some portions of ARPA is a possibility that apparently was recognized by the USFS (Schneider and Beckes 1989:5). As described earlier, ARPA requires the preservation of archaeological resources, including human remains. However, the newly enacted Native American Grave Protection and Repatriation Act may have resolved these potential conflicts in favor of the USFS policy.

This policy provides a test at the federal institutional level of the relative strengths of conflicting values. On one side is the value of respectful treatment of human remains and a growing consideration of aboriginal cultural sensitivities. On the other is the value of enhanced knowledge and scientific advancement for the benefit of the population at large, even where this may prove painful to a minority population's cultural sensitivities.

Issues under the U.S. Constitution

In addition to common law, federal statutes, and policies of federal agencies, the U.S. Constitution plays a central role in moderating conflicts between values. All law in the United States must conform to the Constitution. Four constitutional issues have been raised by commentators and at court in the context of disposition of prehistoric aboriginal remains and grave goods. These include the interplay between the freedom of religion and establishment of religion clauses, the prohibition against taking of property without compensation, and the equal protection clause as it applies to both Indians and scientists. Some issues involve state legislation, but because they fall under the ambit of the Constitution, they are included here.

Freedom of Religion and the Establishment Clause

As discussed above, AIRFA does not grant substantive rights to Indians in addition to those contained in the First Amendment. That amendment guarantees to individuals the right of free exercise of religion, but acts expressing those beliefs are subject to reasonable government intervention. Indian religious practice often revolves around sacred sites, such as the Black Hills of South Dakota or Kootenai Falls in Idaho. These sites might be employed for individual spiritual vision quests or for complex group rituals (O'Brien 1988:vii–x). Cases involving sacred sites (especially the *Lyng* decision previously described) hold that the landowner, including the federal government, may proceed with actions pertaining to the land even where those actions substantially impair religious practice. The test appears to be that the action may not be purposively designed to prohibit religious practices.

It is suggested (Bowman 1989:175) that some aborigines could present claims that curation of aboriginal remains and grave goods violates their freedom to exercise their religion because of the strong belief of some aborigines that unburied bodies are not at rest until there is total decomposition of the remains. Such a claim, as Bowman and others recognize, could run afoul of the establishment clause of the First Amendment, which prohibits state or federal action that discriminates in favor of or against any religious system. The government may not be hostile to any religion or to the advocacy of no-religion, and it may not aid or promote one religion against another (*Epperson v Arkansas*, S.Ct. 1968). Disposition of aboriginal remains or grave goods on the basis of religious beliefs, especially when the claimants do not otherwise enjoy standing at law, may be considered a violation of the establishment clause. That issue was raised in court in the California case of *People v Van Horn*. The appellate court held that the particular fact situation in that case did not constitute a violation of the establishment clause. However, the issue remains contentious and will no doubt provoke further judicial consideration.

The Native American Rights Fund argues strongly for a liberal interpretation of the Constitution in these cases (Quick 1985:134–36). However, the weight of the decisions and the arguments presented by the commentators cause concern that the establishment clause of the Constitution might present a barrier to repatriation by the governments of aboriginal remains and artifacts on purely religious grounds.

Taking of Property without Compensation

Some state unmarked burial statutes (e.g., Missouri and Minnesota) apply to private property. In general, the statutes provide that ground-disturbing activity that might affect a real or suspected burial must cease until appropriate disposition of the remains is determined and implemented by the state historical preservation officer (Price 1989a:1). This may interfere with commercial use of the property, as was specifically contemplated by the Missouri statute, which prohibits development or agricultural use of the affected property. Under Supreme Court decisions in two 1987 companion cases (*Nollan v California Coastal Commission* and *First English Evangelical Church v Los Angeles*), the court held that a temporary taking for a valid state purpose may require compensation to the landowner under the theory of inverse condemnation. The full implications at law of the decisions are not yet resolved. However, the thrust of the decisions is that the state, in enacting valid state policies for the public good, cannot impose the bulk of the cost of those policies on the property owner. Instead, all citizens must share in the cost through compensation to the landowner from the state's coffers.

Subsequent cases in lower federal courts have apparently narrowed these decisions to apply to interference with commercial use of property (e.g., *Citizen's Association of Portland v International Raceways, Inc.* 1987). It has also been suggested, though never tested at court, that the remains and grave goods located on private land might be considered property and their confiscation and subsequent reburial or repatriation by the state might constitute a taking of property for which compensation must be paid to the property owner (Higginbotham 1982:111–12).

One related case arose in Minnesota (*Thompson, et al. v City of Red Wing* 1990). At the trial court, arguments were pressed under both the state and federal constitutions for compensation in consequence of interference with commercial use of claimants' property—they were not allowed to dig a gravel pit in which burials were located. The lower court did not address the U.S. Constitution but decided the action solely on the basis of the state constitution. The trial court required the state to purchase from the plaintiffs approximately 19.7 acres, which the plaintiffs valued at $871,000, and to pay plaintiffs' court costs and attorney fees in the amount of $24,000.

On appeal, the lower decision was reversed. The state court of appeals held that the claims for compensation were not ripe for adjudication because no final state action had been taken with respect to the land in question. The owners had not submitted a development plan and had proven unresponsive to the state's attempts to mitigate impact and formulate alternative development plans.

The appellate court also described the taking as an "arbitration" function rather than an action of state enterprise. That is, the state was held to be arbitrating between competing uses of the property and not to be taking the property in furtherance of a state enterprise. Thus, said the court, the appropriate question is not whether there was a diminution in property value, but whether the statute deprives the owners of all reasonable use of their property. As the owners continued in their previous agricultural and residential use of the land, the court held that there was no compensable taking in this particular case.

Because of the pivotal issue of ripeness and the limitation to the specific facts of this case, the decision is not dispositive—even in Minnesota—of future claims based on inverse condemnation. However, the case does illustrate some of the considerations involved in this issue.

Equal Protection

The equal protection clause of the Fourteenth Amendment provides that no state shall deny to any person within its jurisdiction the equal protection of law. Although this stricture specifically applies to the states, it has been held to be similarly applicable to the federal government through the Fifth Amendment's "due process" clause. Aborigines might base an equal protection argument on the premise that archaeological efforts have concentrated on aboriginal sites and that state burial and cemetery laws distinguish in practice, if not in intent, between contemporary European-American remains and prehistoric aboriginal remains. An additional argument is that the laws are inherently prejudicial because of their historical evolution. Accordingly, it is impossible to obtain equal treatment (to that given non-aboriginal remains) of aboriginal remains disposed of in traditional aboriginal manner.

However, these issues have not been addressed directly by judicial decision, and the outcome is uncertain. Only in a Supreme Court dissent (J. Black in *Rice v Sioux City Memorial Park Cemetery*, at 80, 1955) has suggestion been offered that unequal treatment of human remains by the government might give rise to issues of equal protection. Further, the ever-present issue of standing is also involved here: Who may object on behalf of prehistoric aborigines?

Complaints under the equal-protection clause are also heard from another quarter, the scientific profession. In the previously cited California case of *People v Van Horn*, archaeologist Van Horn contended unsuccessfully that he and all archaeologists are deprived unconstitutionally by the California reburial law of the ability to pursue their profession because the law requires reburial in accordance with modern Indian religious beliefs. He argued that the due process clauses of the Fifth and Fourteenth Amendments include the word "liberty," and that the concept of liberty includes the right to pursue a lawful occupation. The court was not convinced.

Although the plaintiff did not raise the issue, he might have drawn on the gist of decisions pertaining to taking of property without compensation. Here, he would argue that unreasonable abridgement of the pursuit of his occupation imposes on him and his profession an inequitable portion of the cost of the state policy regarding treatment of aboriginal remains. Therefore, he might argue that he is entitled to compensation for that interference in order to apportion more equitably the cost of the policy among the state's taxpayers.

Once more there is a conflict in values, in this instance values involving the power of the state to enact public policies, the respect for the freedom of a minority group to pursue religious beliefs, the ability of the individual to pursue a profession without unreasonable interference from the state, the advancement of knowledge and science, and the respectful treatment of human remains. Amidst this conflict, the U.S. Constitution is a moderating influence that requires the players in the issue to consider and balance a variety of competing values.

Prohibition against Vague Statutory Language

The due-process clause of the Fourteenth Amendment requires that a statute which forbids or requires an act must be sufficiently clear in its language that men of common intelligence are not required to guess at its meaning and thus differ as to its application (*Giaccio v Pennsylvania*, S.Ct. 1966). In the California case of *People v Van Horn*, defendant Van Horn contended (again unsuccessfully) that the law is unconstitutionally vague for several reasons. First, no definition exists of "associated grave goods." Is material used as mortuary fill and void of other significance to be considered "associated grave goods?" In the Van Horn case, the defendant alleged that two broken pieces of metates found in a grave were not from the same metate, did not show evidence of exhaustive prior use, and carried no religious or cultural significance other than use as convenient fill, along with rocks and dirt. Second, the term "native American" is vague and undefined. Does it include prehistoric residents of what is now Mexico? Defendant contended that at least one of the two individuals found in the grave in question was of Mexican origin. Third, the requisite nature of the belief held by the Native American Heritage Commission that particular individuals are related to the deceased is unclear. No statutory guidelines define the requisite elements of this belief.

Defendant Van Horn contended that belief possibly founded on speculation provides insufficient notice to the defendant and others of the statute's operation. He also complained that the terms "grave" and "burial" require precise definition because of their confusion in other areas of the law. Although these arguments failed under the fact situation presented in California, similar arguments involving different facts, statutory language, and jurisdictions may have stronger prospects for success at court.

Summary of Federal Statutes and Cases

Statutes

Administrative Procedures Act of 1966. 5 U.S.C. 701.
American Indian Religious Freedom Act of 1978. 42 U.S.C. Sect. 1996.
Antiquities Act of 1906. 16 U.S.C. Sect. 431–33.
Archaeological Resources Protection Act. 16 U.S.C. Sect. 470aa–470ll.
Department of Transportation Act of 1966. 49 U.S.C. Sect. 1653.
Historic Sites Act of 1935. 16 U.S.C. Sect. 461–67.
National Environmental Policy Act of 1969. 42 U.S.C. Sect. 4321–70.
National Historic Preservation Act of 1966. 16 U.S.C. Sect. 470–470w.

National Museum of the American Indian Act. P.L. 101-85 [S. 978], 28 November 1989.
Native American Grave Protection and Repatriation Act of 1990. P.L. 101–601, 104 Stat. 3048, 16 November 1990.
Reservoir Salvage Act of 1960. 16 U.S.C. Sect. 462(b).
Surface Mining Control and Reclamation Act of 1977. 30 U.S.C. Sect. 1201–1328.

Cases

A.I.A.D., et al., v AMREP Southwest, Inc. (No. CIV-86-0815 D. N.M. 1986) (unreported).
Citizen's Association of Portland v International Raceways, Inc., 833 F.2d 760 (9th Cir. 1987).
Epperson v Arkansas, 21 L.Ed.2d 228, 89 S.Ct. 266 (1968).
First English Evangelical Lutheran Church of Glendale v County of Los Angeles County, California, 96 L.Ed.2d 250, 107 S.Ct. 2378 (1987).
Giaccio v Pennsylvania, 15 L.Ed.2d 447, 86 S.Ct. 518 (1966).
Indian Lookout Alliance v Volpe, 345 F.Supp. 1167 (S.D. Iowa 1972).
Lyng v Northwest Indian Cemetery Protective Ass'n, 108 S. Ct. 319 (1988).
James Patrick Nollan, et ux, Appellant v California Coastal Commission, 97 L.Ed.2d 677, 107 S.Ct. 3141 (1987).
Rice v Sioux City Memorial Park Cemetery, 349 U.S. 70 (1955).
United States v Diaz, 368 F.Supp. 856 (D. Ariz. 1973), Rev'd, 499 F.2d 113 (9th Cir. 1974).

4   State Law

All states have laws that address in some manner the disposition of prehistoric aboriginal remains and grave goods. Some merely apply their criminal laws against grave robbing, trespass, and vandalism, or their general public health and cemetery laws (Price 1989b:1–2). Increasingly, states have implemented legislation specific to the problem. There is little consistency in approach. Differences among the states may be due to disparities in any number of variables: the degree of public consciousness about the values at issue, whether there is a modal consensus on a proper balance between competing values, the presence and relative visibility of resident aboriginal groups, the history of a pre-contact sedentary aboriginal population to deposit remains and grave goods, the relevant values held by resident aboriginal populations, and the time necessary to test new laws in practice against values with which they might compete.

The applicable state laws are considered below in alphabetical order, with a list of relevant statutes, cases, and other documents following each analysis.

Alabama

Alabama has no laws that specifically pertain to reburial or repatriation of prehistoric aboriginal remains or grave goods. Two statutes deal with antiquities, both dictating preservation of archaeological material.

The Alabama Antiquities Act (41-3-1, et seq.) was enacted in 1915 and was ostensibly designed to prevent plundering of Alabama's archaeological resources by archaeological institutions from outside the state. The text is unclear and to the best of the author's knowledge has never been tested in court. In essence, it provides that the state reserves exclusive right to explore, excavate, and survey all aboriginal mounds, earthworks, and burial sites located within Alabama, subject to the rights of owners of private land upon which the antiquities are located for agricultural, domestic, or industrial purposes. It continues with the assertion that objects located within any of these sites are the property of the state.

Subsequent provisions are confusing. Nonresidents of Alabama are not allowed to explore or excavate any of the sites either directly or through an agent. However, private landowners may give consent for such work, and objects removed are retained by the state. Violations are punished by a fine of up to $1,000.

The second specific statute (41-9-240, et seq.) establishes the Alabama Historical Commission. The Commission is charged with preserving the historical heritage of the state, a task which includes excavating, protecting, and interpreting archaeological sites. Again, the emphasis is on preservation.

There are a variety of cemetery laws (11-47-60, et seq.), laws dealing with the treatment of dead bodies (22-19-01, et seq.), public decency laws dealing with the mistreatment of corpses (13A-11-13), and laws prohibiting desecration of venerated objects, including burials (13A-11-12). However, these laws do not appear to apply to prehistoric aboriginal remains or grave goods. The statutory text applies to cemeteries established in the modern sense. And the definition of body probably follows the Ohio rule that completely decomposed skeletal remains, and especially those of prehistoric individuals, are not considered skeletons in the meaning of the criminal statutes. Furthermore, a relatively liberal test for abandonment of cemeteries was announced (*Boyd v Brabham*). The court cited with approval the rule that even when bodies remain in place, the cemetery may be considered abandoned if additional interments cannot be made, have not been made for a long time, grave markers have lost their identity, and the site is no longer treated as a cemetery by the public.

The Alabama Historical Commission recognizes the deficiencies in the state laws. It is now studying the experience of other states to guide recommendations to the state legislature for the preparation of new legislation (Brooms 1989).

Statutes

Ala. Code 11-47-60, et seq., Cemeteries and Burial Grounds.
Ala. Code 13A-11-13, Abuse of Corpse.
Ala. Code 22-19-1, et seq., Dead Bodies.
Ala. Code 41-31-1, et seq., Aboriginal Mounds, Earthworks, and Other Antiquities.
Ala. Code 41-9-240, et seq., Alabama Historical Commission.

Cases

Boyd v Brabham, et al., 414 SO.2d 931 (Ala. S.Ct. 1982).

Alaska

Alaska presents an amalgam of specific statutory protection, application of general criminal and health laws to prehistoric aboriginal remains, and cooperative efforts with local aboriginal communities. The specific statute (41.35.200, et seq.) is oriented toward preservation. However, it does specifically recognize cultural rights and responsibilities of aborigines, and a limited repatriation to them of some objects. It also (41.35.020b) provides that if a local cultural group has adequate curatorial facilities and practices, it may obtain from the state custody of artifacts and other items of significance to them for study or display. If the objects are not properly maintained, they must be returned to the state.

The statute does not appear to apply to objects found on private land, but specifically applies only to land owned or controlled by the state (41.35.020). However, the office of the state attorney general advises that the issue of who owns archaeological resources in the state remains an open question (Mertz 1989). Archaeological excavation is by permit from the commissioner of the Department of Natural Resources to qualified institutions and then only if the results will be made known to the public through institutions and museums. However, if the archaeological resource is of sacred or religious significance to a cultural group, the consent of that group must be obtained before the permit will be issued (41.35.080). To the best of the author's knowledge, this provision has not been tested under the establishment clause of the U.S. Constitution. Criminal penalties include a penalty of a fine of up to $1,000 and imprisonment of up to six months. In addition, a civil penalty may also be assessed of up to $100,000 for each violation (41.35.215).

Dovetailing with the Historic Preservation Act is the coroner's enabling legislation (12.65.020–.040). Alaska is reported to consider all human remains in an archaeological context as "dead bodies" for purposes of this statute (Smith 1984:145–46). The practice in the state appears to be that the coroner assumes jurisdiction over all remains. If there is no surviving spouse or next of kin, the coroner authorizes necessary and reasonable scientific examination of the remains with the advice of the state archaeologist and is responsible for ensuring subsequent reburial with the cooperation of the appropriate municipality or village.

The office of the attorney general advises that there is no real controversy in Alaska regarding disposition of human remains (Mertz 1989). Rather, the contentious issue is disposition of artifacts. Pending litigation (*Chilkat Indian Village v Johnson,* unreported) involves the sale of the Tlingit "rain screen" from the Whale House in Klukwan. A group of villagers removed the screen for sale to an out-of-state collector. Because a recipient of property takes no better title than was held by the transferor, stolen property must revert to the rightful owner. In the present case, determination of legal right to dispose of the screen is an issue to be decided under tribal law.

In 1984 the state commenced criminal proceedings and the village council sued the villagers who removed the screen and an intermediate art dealer who was also involved. The actions are still at a very early stage and involve the complex issues of which villagers have the right to possess the screen under traditional Tlingit law, whether any villagers may sell it without approval of all members of the clan, whether the village council may prescribe rules for its disposition, and which courts—state or federal—have jurisdiction over the controversy. The lawsuits are only now at the point of resolving the issue of jurisdiction.

Statutes

Alaska Stat. 12.65.010, et seq., Coroners.
Alaska Stat. 41.35.010, et seq., Alaska Historic Preservation Act.

Cases

Chilkat Indian Village v Johnson (unreported, Dist. Ct. 1989).

Arizona

As in most other states, the Arizona statutes mandate preservation of archaeological resources and do not address repatriation of resources to aborigine claimants. Policies and implementing regulations grant more aboriginal participation in the decision-making process regarding disposition of remains than is required by the state law. These statutes do not control archaeological resources located on private property.

The Arizona Antiquities Act (41-841, et seq.) provides that, except by authority of permit, no one may excavate archaeological sites or collect archaeological specimens on land owned or controlled by the state. An archaeological specimen is defined as any item resulting from past human life (including human skeletal material) that is at least one hundred years old. Only educational institutions, public museums, and nonprofit scientific and research corporations may obtain permits. Permits are issued by the director of the Arizona State Museum, who has discretion over the duration of the permit's validity and the purposes for which it may be employed. There are also statutes prohibiting both forgery and vandalism of archaeological resources (13-3702). Collections made in violation of the statute can incur penalties of up to five years' imprisonment and a fine of up to $150,000 (13-701, 13-801).

By regulations effected to implement the statute (12-6-101–12-6-714), the permittee must attempt to identify relatives of individuals whose remains are discovered by the permittee. Failing this, the permittee must attempt to identify specific living groups or common cultural groups with affinity to the decedent. Specific notice of the discovery must be given to these individuals or to their representatives (tribal governing bodies in the event of Indian tribes). If no cultural affiliation is found, notice of the remains must be published in general circulation newspapers in the state capital and the county where the remains are located. Advice from affiliated living groups is solicited and considered by the director of the state museum, who finally determines the manner of disposition.

The state museum also has a policy stating that the museum will treat the remains of all people with the same high degree of respect. Accordingly, the museum avoids excavation or analysis of human remains found on Indian land unless the prior permission of the appropriate tribal government is obtained. Disinterment may be assisted by tribal religious representatives. Remains threatened with destruction may be removed with the assistance of tribal officials and religious representatives. Any analysis will be conducted in a timely manner and remains will be ultimately disposed of as agreed with tribal representatives. The relationship of the policy to the ARPA provisions, discussed earlier, is unclear. The policy may operate to limit Indian rights otherwise provided under ARPA, though this is a very tentative conclusion and requires further study.

The Arizona Historic Preservation Act (41-861, et seq.) establishes the state Historic Preservation Office. The office is charged with identification, evaluation, and protection of Arizona's prehistoric and historic cultural resources. Among other things, it is also responsible for rehabilitation of archaeological sites and objects that are publicly owned or owned by a nonprofit organization and that are listed in the Arizona or National Register of Historic Places (41-881).

The intent of the laws is to preserve archaeological resources on state land. Repatriation is not contemplated. By regulation and policy, recognition is made of Indian sensitivity toward Indian remains. Advice of Indian representatives is sought and considered, and tribal approval for disposition of remains on Indian land must be obtained.

Statutes

Ariz. Rev. Stat. Ann. 13-701, et seq., and 13-801, et seq., Criminal Penalties.
Ariz. Rev. Stat. Ann. 13-3702, et seq., Defacing or Damaging Petroglyphs, etc.
Ariz. Rev. Stat. Ann. 41-841, et seq., Arizona Antiquities Act.
Ariz. Rev. Stat. Ann. 41-861, et seq., Arizona Historic Preservation Act.
Ariz. Rev. Stat. Ann. 41-881, et seq., Historic Property Rehabilitation.

Other Documents

Arizona State Museum Policy, approved 2 February 1985.
Regulations Governing the Arizona State Museum, 12-6-101–12-6-714, effective 8 October 1985.

Arkansas

The state has no statutes that specifically address repatriation of items to aborigine claimants or reburial of prehistoric human remains. Draft legislation was considered in 1987, but it failed in committee (House Bill 1047). It is the policy of the state historic preservation officer to refer interested parties to the guidelines of the federal government's Advisory

Council on Historic Preservation for the treatment of human remains (Buford 1989). The role of the Historic Preservation Program and the state Historic Preservation Office is limited to non-archaeological functions, except to the extent necessary to cooperate with the Arkansas Archaeological Survey (13-7-106), which has jurisdiction over archaeological functions.

The Arkansas antiquities statutes (13-6-201, et seq.) do not apply to private property except to the extent that state policy discourages private, unsupervised excavation (13-6-301b). The state declares ownership of all archaeological resources located on land owned or controlled by the state. The definition of "site" as an archaeological resource includes burial grounds, and the definition of "artifacts" as items found in sites includes aboriginal relics (13-6-302).

The president of the University of Arkansas is designated the agent of the state for purposes of archaeological research and is responsible for appointing the state archaeologist, who administers the archaeological programs. Excavation of ruins and mounds is required under the statute (13-6-202-1), and to the extent possible, items recovered must be made available for scientific use and public display (13-6-213b). Violation of the statutes constitutes a misdemeanor with potential fines of from $50 to $500 and incarceration from one to six months (13-6-303).

Arkansas has typical statutes relating to abuse of corpses, removal of bodies, and opening graves (5-60-101, et seq.). The same problems with the applicability of these laws to completely decomposed aboriginal remains in unmarked graves arise here. It is unclear if an unmarked prehistoric burial constitutes a grave for purposes of the criminal statutes, and (as in Ohio) a decomposed skeleton of a prehistoric aborigine may not be considered a body. There is little consideration given at law in Arkansas to cultural sensitivities of living aborigines.

Statutes

Ark. Stat. Ann. 5-60-101, et seq., Abuse of a Corpse.
Ark. Stat. Ann. 13-6-201, et seq., Archaeological Research.
Ark. Stat. Ann. 13-7-106, Historic Preservation Program.

California

Prompted by increased looting and vandalism of Indian burials and monuments, and by the example of dramatic cases such as *Wana the Bear v Community Construction, Inc.*, California has enacted one of the most sweeping and severe "unmarked burial" laws in the nation. The laws apply to both public and private property and provide that in the event of the discovery of human remains in a location other than a dedicated cemetery, the county coroner is to be notified (7050.5). If the coroner lacks jurisdiction over the remains and they are of "Native American" origin, the coroner notifies the Native American Heritage Commission (NAHC), a state agency, of the existence and identity of the remains.

When the NAHC receives notice, it contacts those persons it believes to be most likely descended from the decedent (5097.98). With the permission of the property owner, the descendants may then examine the site and recommend means for treating or disposing of the remains and associated grave goods with appropriate dignity. If no descendant is identified, or the descendants fail to make a recommendation, or the landowner rejects the recommendation, the landowner must rebury the remains and associated grave goods at a site not subject to further disturbance. Furthermore, no person may obtain or possess native American artifacts or remains taken from a grave or cairn on or after January 1, 1984, except as otherwise provided at law or pursuant to an agreement worked out with the landowner. Violations of this law constitute a felony punishable by imprisonment in the state prison (5097.99). This is also the penalty for most other types of mutilation or removal of corpses (7051; 7052).

The statute has been questioned at court. The issues of conflict with the establishment of religion, equal protection, and void for vagueness clauses of the U.S. Constitution are discussed in that portion of chapter 3 addressing constitutional issues, particularly in the context of the California case of *People v Van Horn*. To the best of the author's knowledge, the statute has not been tested under the Constitutional prohibition against taking property without compensation. The statute emphasizes respectful treatment of aboriginal remains and considers aboriginal sensitivities, but it is not without problems.

Finally, there reportedly has been voluntary repatriation of Indian remains beyond the scope required by the statute (Mathews 1989). Stanford University has agreed to return the skeletal remains of approximately 525 Indians to their descendants, the Ohlone-Costanoan tribe.

Stanford may request retention of some skeletal materials for further study, but this decision will rest with the tribe.

Statutes

Cal. Public Resources Code, Sect. 5097.9, et seq.
Cal. Health and Safety Code, Sect. 7050.5.

Cases

The People of the State of California, et al., v David Van Horn, et al., 267 Cal. Rptr. 804 (Cal. App. 4 Dist. 1990).
Wana the Bear v Community Construction, Inc., 128 Cal. App. 3d 536 (Cal. 1982).

Colorado

The state Historic Preservation Act (24-80-405) is a preservation statute applicable to state but not to private lands. The act is administered through the state Historical Society by the state archaeologist. The state declares exclusive right to exploit archaeological resources on state land, except that excavation permits may be issued to qualified entities by the state archaeologist. The state archaeologist is charged with the duty of collecting and preserving archaeological resources. Those who excavate on state land without authority of a permit are subject to a fine of up to $500 and imprisonment for up to thirty days.

The general statute prohibiting the abuse of a corpse (18-13-101) has been determined by the office of the state attorney general to be applicable to prehistoric aboriginal remains (Clouse 1979). This statute provides that anyone who removes human remains from a grave or who treats these remains in any way that would outrage normal family sensibilities is guilty of a class 2 misdemeanor. If the state archaeologist determines that aboriginal remains located on private property are threatened by improper treatment, the office of the attorney general can obtain a temporary restraining order against any such action, citing violation of the abuse of corpse statute.

Practical administration of the statutes has resulted in procedures developed by the Colorado Historical Society in cooperation with the Colorado Native American Heritage Council (CNAH) to govern the reinterment of ancient native American skeletal remains. The policy does not apply to contemporary remains or to a process of cemetery reloca-tion. When ancient Indian remains are discovered, and if the state archaeologist has jurisdiction and determines the procedure to be applica-ble, the CNAH is notified and given opportunity to comment on excava-tion, analysis, and ultimate disposition of the remains.

Remains linked to specific tribes will be offered to those tribes for appropriate disposition. Indian remains which cannot be so associated will be given to the CNAH for curation at the University of Colorado museum until they are reburied. The CNAH has use of property at Golden Gate Canyon State Park for this purpose. Requests for study of the remains prior to reburial must be addressed to the CNAH. In general there is only one reburial ceremony per year. Clearly, the procedure is more considerate of Indian sensitivities and affords more participation by the Indian community in the process than does the statutory framework.

Statutes

Colo. Rev. Stat. 18-13-101, Abuse of a Corpse.
Colo. Rev. Stat. 24-80-401, et seq., Historical, Prehistorical, and Ar-chaeological Resources.

Other Documents

Colorado Historical Society Procedure Governing the Reinterment of Native American Remains, 1987.

Connecticut

The state enacted an unmarked burial law in 1989 (Public Act 89-368). Regulations have not yet been drafted, and there is no operating experience under the law, so it is difficult to determine the precise operation of the new legislation. The law applies both to private and public lands, and to grave goods as well as human remains. In a limited sense, it contemplates repatriation of some items to Indian representatives.

Definitions are precise and avoid the problems of vagueness in the text that are evident in the statutes of some other states. The law applies to sites, objects, and remains older than fifty years. It establishes the Native American Heritage Advisory Council which makes recommendations on Indian materials to the state Historical Commission (established under 10-321) and to the state archaeologist. The council is comprised of members from each of the tribes recognized by the state, the Indian Affairs Council, and nominees of various other entities. The state recognizes five tribes and has five reservations (Poirier et al. 1985:6).

The new law charges the Historical Commission with the identification and inventory of sacred and archaeological sites within the state and with the adoption of regulations for their preservation. The commission is given permitting authority for excavation on state lands, and no excavation can take place without such a permit. The law also establishes a state museum to serve as the repository for all materials discovered during archaeological investigations on state land. Interestingly, the museum is required to establish a policy that allows the loan and transfer of sacred objects and other materials to native American museums.

When human burials or skeletal remains are discovered, the medical examiner and the state archaeologist are notified. If the remains have been buried longer than fifty years, the state archaeologist takes jurisdiction. If the remains are Indian, the Native American Heritage Advisory Council is also notified and consulted. If the remains are on private property, the state archaeologist has seventy-two hours to come to agreement with the landowner for preservation, *in situ*, or reburial of the remains.

The landowner bears none of the cost for disposition of the remains. There is no provision for consequences in the event agreement cannot be reached. However, it is unlikely that the landowner will be allowed to disturb the remains if they are left in place. A further section of the act provides that no person is allowed to engage in any activity that might disturb or alter any native American burial or sacred site without benefit of a permit from the state Historical Commission. There is no stated exception for sites on private property. Penalties include a fine of up to $5,000 or twice the value of artifacts and cost of restoration of the site, whichever is greater, and imprisonment for up to five years.

There are also various other provisions, including statements formally recognizing several tribes and contemplating the impact on native American and archaeological sites by state projects. Questions of taking private property without compensation occur, although this is difficult to assess in the absence of published operating regulations. The law considers preservation, respectful treatment of human remains, and a limited repatriation of items in the form of transfers and loans to native American museums. Scientific analysis of remains is allowed without a fixed statutory time limitation, and Indian participation in the process is assured from the time the state archaeologist is first notified. A cooperative relationship among Indian groups and the various agencies was established prior to the act (Poirier et al. 1985:10), and the attorney general's office reports that there is no known litigation under the legislation prior to the new act (Kwanashie 1989).

Statutes

Public Act No. 89-368, Act Implementing the Recommendations of the Task Force on Indian Affairs.
Conn. Gen. Stat. Ann. 10-321, et seq., Connecticut Historical Commission.

Delaware

The applicable Delaware statute (5403, et seq.) applies to all public and private land in the state, excluding federal property. Reportedly, the statute was prompted by the Island Field site in South Bowers, Delaware (anon. 1987). The site is a prehistoric Indian cemetery containing the remains of 127 individuals. Archaeologists had excavated the site and placed artifacts on display in cases and the skeletal remains on display, *in situ,* much to the irritation of the local Nanticoke tribe, which successfully campaigned for remedial legislation.

The statute only applies to skeletal material and does not address issues of grave goods or other artifacts. It is quite simple. All human remains in the state which were above ground as of the effective date of the legislation (the act was effective in 1987) were to be reinterred within one year. For newly discovered native American remains that do not come under the jurisdiction of the medical examiner, the matter is referred to a committee comprised of the chief of the Nanticoke tribe, two members appointed by him, the director of the Division of Historical and Cultural Affairs of the Department of State, two members appointed by the director, and a seventh member from the private sector appointed by the governor.

The committee is notified within five days of the discovery of native American remains. Sixty days thereafter the director advises the committee of a plan for disposition of the remains. Reinterment must take place within ninety days of discovery unless the committee grants an extension. Penalties are severe: fines of from $1,000 to $10,000 and imprisonment for up to two years.

All remains from Delaware museums and other repositories, including the Island Field site, are reported to have been reinterred by June 3, 1988. They were reburied in air tight containers to allow researchers to exhume them for further research, upon receipt of consent of the committee. Prior to reburial, samples were taken for future analysis, again with the committee's consent (Ubelaker and Grant 1989:276).

The legislation protects values pertaining to respectful treatment of human remains, and it considers aboriginal sensitivities by including Indian representatives in the decision-making process. The impact on educational and scientific values is yet to be determined; in large part, this will be a function of the attitudes and decisions of the committee. Questions regarding disposition of cultural artifacts remain unanswered.

Statutes

Del. Code Ann. 5403, et seq., Archaeological Excavation.

Florida

The state pursues a policy of preserving archaeological resources through the Historic Preservation Advisory Council and the Division of Historical Resources (267.011, et seq.). That division employs the state archaeologist and the state historic preservation officer. The state archaeologist is responsible for administering the statute pertaining to unmarked burials (872.06, et seq.).

The state statutes pertaining to offenses concerning dead bodies and graves (872.01, et seq.) and those involving cemeteries (497.005, et seq.)

apply equally to aboriginal remains. However, this protection may not prove especially useful for traditional Indian inhumations, even those of contemporary decedents. In *Newman v State*, the Florida District Court of Appeals held that the removal of a contemporary Seminole skull by a college student from an unmarked traditional grave in the Everglades did not violate the state desecration statutes because the taking was not malicious, per se, and there was no evidence of malice.

The unmarked burial statute applies to private lands, as well as to associated grave goods, and to all remains of individuals who have been deceased for at least seventy-five years and that are not covered by the criminal or cemetery statutes. When remains are found that are in excess of the seventy-five-year period and the medical examiner determines that he does not have jurisdiction, disposition of the remains falls to the state archaeologist. All ground-disturbing work in the vicinity of the remains must cease until otherwise authorized by the medical examiner or the state archaeologist. A skeletal analyst or the supervising archaeologist (in the event the remains are discovered in the course of an archaeological excavation) is obliged to make a report to the state archaeologist on the cultural and biological characteristics of the remains.

If the remains are considered by the state archaeologist to be scientifically, archaeologically, or historically important, there will be no reinterment until the remains are analyzed by the skeletal analyst. The state archaeologist is required to locate and contact the nearest relation or ethnic community affiliated with the decedent. If this is impossible, the archaeologist consults a committee comprised of a skeletal analyst, two native Americans if the remains are those of native Americans, two members of the ethnic group affiliated with the decedent if not native American, and an individual with special expertise in the particular type of unmarked burial involved.

If the state archaeologist deems the remains to be scientifically significant and the members of the committee agree, the remains and the artifacts shall belong to the state with title vested in the Division of Historical Resources. Of special interest is a provision that requires archaeologists who conduct excavations of sites containing human remains to publish full reports within two years from completion of the excavation (872.05[7]). Penalties for violations of the statute are severe, progressing up to those for a felony in the third degree.

The statute is reported to work well in protecting remains and sites that contain them. However, due to lack of funds, there is little that is done to mitigate impact on sites, to analyze remains, or to curate or reinter remains and artifacts (Scarry 1989). Among other questions is what occurs if the committee members do not agree with the state archaeologist that the remains and the artifacts should be owned by the state. Issues similar to those raised in the Van Horn case in California also appear to be present here: What is a "native American?" What are associated burial artifacts?

Constitutional issues about taking private property without compensation appear to be present. This is relevant in the confiscation of artifacts found on private land and in interference with commercial use of private property until the medical examiner or the state archaeologist resolve the manner for disposition of the remains. Some of these questions will no doubt test the statute.

Statutes

Fla. St. Ann. 267.011, et seq., Florida Historical Resources Act.
Fla. St. Ann. 497.500, et seq., Cemeteries.
Fla. St. Ann. 872.01, et seq., Offenses Concerning Dead Bodies and Graves.
Fla. St. Ann. 872.05, Unmarked Human Burials.

Cases

Newman v State, 174 So.2d 479 (Fla. Dist. Ct. App. 1965).

Georgia

Georgia laws do not consider reburial or repatriation of prehistoric aboriginal remains or grave goods. The emphasis is on preservation, and these laws pertain only to land owned or controlled by the state, except that the state urges that archaeological excavation on private property be undertaken solely by recognized scientific institutions or qualified individuals (12-3-52d).

The state has established the Department of Archives and History, whose primary responsibility is the collection, dissemination, and preservation of significant historical data on Georgia (45-13-40, et seq.). It has the additional function of preserving and fostering the culture and heritage of Indians within the state. (45-13-43). This section might be used in the context of reburial and repatriation, but to the best of the author's knowledge it has not been so employed, possibly because the department is prohibited from operating in areas administered by other state agencies.

Responsibility for the preservation and excavation of archaeological material lies with the Department of Natural Resources (12-3-50, et seq.). Archaeological excavation on land owned or controlled by the state is the exclusive province of the department, although permits may be issued by the commissioner of natural resources (with the advice of the state archaeologist) to recognized scientific organizations and qualified individuals. Violations constitute a misdemeanor.

The state has the typical panoply of statutes pertaining to disturbance of grave sites (26-1812), abuse of corpse (88-2710, et seq.), criminal trespass (26-1503), and grave disturbance through land development (23-2716). Applicability of these statutes to situations involving prehistoric aboriginal remains is uncertain and will probably depend on the special circumstances of each case.

Actual practice, however, may recognize Indian sensitivities. Reburial of Indian remains in several instances is reported (Ubelaker and Grant 1989:277). In addition, an informal effort is underway to draft specific legislation for presentation to the state general assembly (Frazier 1988:3). Except for the broad mandate to the Department of Archives and History, there is no specific statutory recognition of aboriginal cultural sensitivity regarding prehistoric remains and grave goods. Actual practice may be more responsive to these sensitivities than is apparent from the statutory text.

Statutes

Ga. Code Ann. 12-3-50, et seq., Conservation and Natural Resources.
Ga. Code Ann. 23-2716, Disturbance of Burial Place for Land Development.
Ga. Code Ann. 26-1503, Criminal Trespass.
Ga. Code Ann. 26-1812, Punishment for Removal of Memorials.
Ga. Code Ann. 45-13-40, et seq., Department of Archives and History.
Ga. Code Ann. 88-2710, et seq., Illegal Removal of Dead Body from Grave.

Hawaii

Hawaii's Historic Preservation laws (6E, et seq.) are oriented to preservation and do not specifically apply to grave goods. They apply to private land only in a preliminary manner. However, they do consider native Hawaiian concerns, and they do contemplate reburial of native Hawaiian remains. The Department of Land and Natural Resources is responsible for establishing a comprehensive historic preservation program, including archaeological research and the regulation of archaeological activities throughout the state.

When human remains are discovered, land-disturbing activities in the vicinity must cease, and notification is given to the police and the medical examiner. If the remains are from significant historic or prehistoric burials, the department will assert jurisdiction over them, collect archaeological data, and prepare a mitigation plan that can include the acquisition of more data (6E-43). If the remains are likely to be those of native Hawaiians, the Office of Hawaiian Affairs is notified. The landowner, permittee, or developer is responsible for the execution of the mitigation plan and disposition of the remains. However, allocation of the burden of cost is not addressed. Furthermore, the statute may have an impact on private contracts, for it provides that "down time" incurred as the result of a contractor's compliance with this section does not count against any contractor's completion date agreement (6E-43 [c4]).

If the remains are discovered outside the context of a project, the Department of Land and Natural Resources is responsible for execution of the mitigation plan. If the remains are to be archaeologically removed, the department must consult with representatives of the ethnic group affiliated with the decedent. Disposition may be accompanied by traditional ceremonies, as the group and department deem appropriate. Special disposition requests by lineal descendants shall be conducted at the expense of those descendants.

Extensive regulations implement this statute and are followed in practice, but they have been in draft form since 1987. Among other things, they provide definitions, describe permitting processes, and set out requisite qualifications for permittees. The statute is reported to work well in practice. A number of burial treatment/reinterment plans have been worked out to all parties' satisfaction. All cases except one have undergone osteological analysis, one of which was done at the request of the lineal descendants. In the case without such analysis, the skeletal material was too fragmentary to justify analysis (Nagata 1989).

Hawaii presents one of the most dramatic illustrations of the operation of a state reburial law. A Ritz-Carlton hotel was under development on the island of Maui by the Kapalua Land Company when a native Hawaiian cemetery containing the remains of approximately nine hundred individuals was discovered. Through activity of the Hawaiian activist group Hui Alanui O Makena, operation of the state law, and the goodwill of the parties involved, including the governor, a settlement is reported to be near resolution. The development company has redesigned and relocated the proposed hotel and will maintain the cemetery undisturbed in perpetuity. The state legislature has appropriated $6 million to compensate the company for the attendant expenses, $500,000 of which is to be used for the maintenance of the cemetery (Griffin 1989). There is residual dispute with Hui Alanui O Makena over whether the native Hawaiian remains will undergo further osteological analysis prior to reinterment (Roberson 1988:1).

Some native Hawaiians object to reburial on the basis of loss of archaeological information that could help fill the gaps in their history (Kalima 1989). In consideration of aboriginal sensitivity, priority appears to be given to traditionalists among the native Hawaiian population. As with the Indians, one may ask, "Who speaks for the native Hawaiians?"

Statutes

Haw. Rev. Stat. 6E, et seq., Historic Preservation.

Idaho

The Idaho laws are simple, extensive, and apparently enforced. They apply to private as well as to public land, and to artifacts as well as to human remains. They mandate reburial. Under the statutes, no individual may willfully disturb any cairn or grave (27-501, et seq.). This specifically includes Indian graves. Neither may any individual possess any artifacts or human remains taken from a cairn or grave after January 1, 1984.

For instances in which action is necessary to protect a burial site from foreseeable destruction, exceptions are provided upon notification to the director of the Idaho State Historical Society and to the appropriate

Indian tribe if the site contains Indian remains. Under these circumstances, a professional archaeologist may remove objects and remains, with subsequent reinterment to be conducted under supervision of the appropriate Indian tribe, following scientific study.

If there is no emergency—such as imminent destruction by weather or construction—pertaining to the site and an archaeologist wishes to examine it, notice again must be given to the director and to the appropriate Indian tribe in the vicinity. Excavation may not occur without permission of the tribe, but if no reply is given within sixty days from the date of notice, permission shall be deemed to have been granted. Following scientific examination, all items and remains shall be reinterred at the archaeologist's expense and under the supervision of the Indian tribe.

Penalties for violation are severe. Under a separate statute (18-7028), any person who unlawfully removes any part of any human remains is guilty of a felony and subject to imprisonment for up to five years and a fine of up to $10,000. In addition, apparently as inducement to report and prosecute these crimes, any such miscreant is also liable for civil penalties brought by *any* individual, but only once per violation, including punitive damages, compensation for mental anguish, actual damages, and plaintiff's attorney's fees (27-504).

Even with these provisions, there is reported dissatisfaction among the Indian population. When an Oregon man was convicted of robbing Indian graves and selling the artifacts, he was placed on five years' probation and ordered to pay $11,800 to restore the burial grounds. The punishment is reported to be considered by the Nez Percé as a "slap on the wrist" (anon. 1986). Idaho espouses values that consider aboriginal sensitivity toward Indian remains and grave goods, though some protection is given to education and scientific advance. However, the advantage here is given to Indian control over their remains.

Statutes

Idaho Code 18-7028, et seq., Unlawful Removal of Human Remains.
Idaho Code 27-501, et seq., Protection of Graves.

Illinois

The Illinois Historic Preservation Act (127:133d1, et seq.) is oriented toward preservation. The law establishes a registry of sites of significance to the state. If these are located on private property, they cannot be registered without the consent of the landowner. Damage to a registered site is punishable by a fine of up to $10,000.

The Aboriginal Records and Antiquities Act (137:133c1, et seq.) protects burial sites on state lands. Excavation of these sites cannot be undertaken except under permit issued by the department with authority over the site and with the advice of the Illinois State Museum.

A new "Grave Robbery Act" was enacted in August of 1989. Regulations have not yet been drafted with which to administer the new law, and its practical effect has yet to be tested. In summary, the law prohibits disturbance of any unregistered grave over one hundred years old, including associated grave goods, without benefit of an excavation permit issued by the state Historic Preservation Agency. This includes graves located on private property. Violators incur fines of up to $10,000 and imprisonment for up to one year. Civil damages may also be imposed and the Historic Preservation Agency is authorized to offer rewards of up to $2,000 for reports of violations of the act.

Other laws which might apply are the coroners statute (31:10) and a law against removal of bodies (31:10.5). However, the first law is sufficiently narrowly phrased that it probably would not be useful. The removal-of-bodies statute provides that there shall be no removal of a body or associated property from the place of death without a permit from the coroner, unless such removal was necessary to protect the body. By informal letter opinion given in 1981, the office of the state attorney general advised that these statutes probably are not applicable to prehistoric aboriginal remains (Denney 1981).

The Illinois legislature is considering two other relevant bills during the 1989 legislative session. One of these would require a formal assessment of potential impact on archaeological resources prior to undertaking state-funded projects (S.B. 0467). Another is a form of antiquities act (H.B. 2664). The Historic Preservation Agency has also issued a policy statement pertaining to disposition of human remains (Devine 1986). When remains are discovered, the preferential treatment is preservation, *in situ*. If this is not possible, cultural groups affiliated with the decedent will be consulted for advice on proper disposition of the remains. As a general rule, reinterment is not contemplated, and remains will be ultimately turned over to the Illinois State Museum for deposition in the human skeleton repository.

Statutes

Ill. Rev. Stat. 31:10, Coroners.
Ill. Rev. Stat. 31:10.5, Removal of Bodies.
Ill. Rev. Stat. 127:133c1, et seq., Aboriginal Records and Antiquities.
Ill. Rev. Stat. 127:133d1, et seq., Illinois Historic Preservation Act.

Other Documents

H.B. 2613, Grave Robberies Act, effective August 1989.
H.B. 2664, Archaeological and Paleontological Resources Protection Act, pending 1989 session.
S.B. 0467, Historic Resources Protection Act, pending 1989 session.

Indiana

The Indiana unmarked burial statute (14-3-3.4-1) was enacted and effective May 8, 1989. Because it is heavily dependent on implementing rules for its administration, and as there has been insufficient time for these rules to be drafted, approved, and tested in practice, details of its operation remain unclear. The law applies to both public and private land, and to artifacts as well as human remains. The act is notable for the activities to which it does not apply. It does not apply, except for the requirement of giving notice of discovery of human remains (14-3-3.4-16), to surface coal mining, agricultural pursuits, surface collecting, or activities governed by the state's cemetery laws (23-14-1-1, et seq.). Apparently, the primary commercial ground-disturbing activity that it will affect is real estate development.

Artifacts, burial objects, and human remains are all defined terms. An artifact is an object made or shaped by human workmanship prior to December 11, 1816. A burial object is any object intentionally placed in a burial ground at or near the time of burial. Human remains are any part of a body at any stage of decomposition, but it does not apply to the remains of individuals who died after December 31, 1939. The act provides that any person who disturbs the ground (this is not restricted to public lands) for purposes of discovering artifacts or burial objects may do so only in accordance with a plan approved by the Department of Natural Resources (DNR). Anyone who disturbs buried human remains must notify the DNR and rebury the remains in a manner and place according to rules adopted by the Natural Resources Commission. Violations are a class A misdemeanor. If an individual while attempting to recover artifacts, burial objects, grave markers, or human remains without an approved plan disturbs buried human remains, a penalty ensues as a class D felony.

When human remains are discovered, all ground disturbing activity must cease—except those activities specifically exempted—until the DNR authorizes continuation or restricts continuation in accordance with an approved plan. The only guidance for the formulation of rules and plans is that the rules must consider the "rights and interests" of landowners, respectful treatment of human remains, the value of history and archaeology, the importance of amateur archaeologists, and applicable laws and ethics.

The question of taking property without compensation immediately arises, especially for land developers who appear to be singled out for special treatment in comparison to miners and farmers. The reference in the rules to the rights and interests of landowners is anomalous in view of the restrictions. However, no mention is made of ownership of the artifacts and burial objects and it may be that the rules to be drafted will leave that ownership with the landowner, but only actual practice will reveal this answer. Human remains are to be reburied, and there is no provision for study of them, except that this might be included in the rules and plans. The statutory definition of burial object also does not answer the question of burial fill raised in the California case of *People v Van Horn.*

Statutes

Ind. Code Ann. 14-3-3.4-1, et seq., Department of Natural Resources.
Ind. Code Ann. 23-14-1-1, et seq., Indiana General Cemetery Act.

Iowa

The Iowa reburial statute has been in place since 1976 and has served as inspiration, if not as a model, for reburial legislation in other states. Administration of the state law is the responsibility of the state archaeologist, who is appointed by the board of regents and is a member of the faculty of the department of anthropology at the University of Iowa (305A, et seq.). The law extends to include prehistoric burial mounds and unmarked cemeteries and presumes ultimate reburial of ancient human remains. These are defined as remains found within the state that are more than 150 years old. Sites are protected and preserved whenever possible. The state archaeologist reports handling sixty-eight projects in thirty-nine counties, in addition to thirteen repository collections, from July 1987 through June 1988 (Green n.d.).

Individuals who find ancient remains are required to contact the state archaeologist. That officer then obtains the report of a physical anthropologist to determine cultural affiliation. If the remains are ancient, as defined, they will be buried in one of three state cemeteries established for that purpose. The state archaeologist has the authority to deny disinterment of human remains even if they are considered to have state or national significance (305A.9).

Although the state archaeologist is required to publish reports (685-6.1), locations and similar details of sites may be kept in confidence if looting is threatened (22.7.21; 305A.10; 685-14.1). Violation of the statutes is considered criminal mischief in the third degree (716.5). The state archaeologist is authorized to issue permits for archaeological excavation to qualified individuals upon their submitting justification of significance. In making determinations, the state archaeologist will consult with an informal advisory committee composed of osteologists, anthropologists, state agency officials, the lay public, and a minimum of two native Americans residing in Iowa (685-11.7).

The statute does not address grave goods, and the office of the state archaeologist maintains a collection of artifacts for study and display. Apparently, the law does apply to private land, as there is no specific restriction to lands owned or controlled by the state. The provision pertaining to the advisory committee appears in the administrative roles and is not required by statute.

The statute is not without published criticism. One complaint is that long-term, problem-oriented research is precluded by the Iowa insistence on reburial (Buikstra 1981:27). Another criticism is that the statute does not appear responsive to Indian concerns because it is said to presume that remains will be disinterred for study prior to ultimate reburial, it does not require consultation with the Indian group most likely affiliated with the decedent, and it requires burial of all remains in a state cemetery regardless of the religious beliefs of the descendants (Bowman 1989: 205–6).

However, the statute is reported to work well in practice (Quick 1985:131–32; Bowman 1989:205–6). It is claimed to have created an environment of trust and enrichment between Indians and archaeologists. The state Indian Advisory Committee is constantly consulted when finds are made and often participates by visiting the sites and providing advice and traditional religious experts (Quick 1985:130–31). The reburial situation in Iowa may be one in which intelligent and considerate implementation and administration of the laws transcends any defects inherent in the statutory text.

Statutes

Iowa Code 22.7.21, Examination of Public Records.
Iowa Code 305A, et seq., State Archaeologist.
Iowa Code 716, et seq., Damage and Trespass to Property.

Other Documents

Iowa Administrative Code 685, Archaeologist.

Kansas

Kansas passed a specific unmarked burial statute in 1989 (H.B. 2144), which was inspired by a reburial symposium held at Haskell Indian Junior College in January 1986 and modeled after the law of Wisconsin (Lees 1988:1). The law becomes effective January 1, 1990 (anon. 1989b:1). It applies to private as well as public land and to artifacts as well as human remains. Regulations are now being drafted for implementing the new law.

After January 1, 1990, no individual without permit may willfully disturb any unmarked burial site, possess human skeletal remains or goods interred with such remains (except that grave goods recovered prior to January 1, 1990, may be privately held), display human remains or associated artifacts from an unmarked burial site, engage in commerce with these articles, or discard any of these materials. Any individual with knowledge of any violation is required by law to report it to the local law enforcement agency. Upon discovery of an unmarked burial site, immediate report is to be made to the local law enforcement authority, which contacts either the coroner or the state Historical Society, as appropriate. Following this notification, reference is made to the state archaeologist and to the newly created Unmarked Burial Sites Preservation Review Board.

Penalties for primary violations are severe. A sequence of graduated fines is imposed with a potential fine of up to $100,000, plus a potential civil penalty of up to $2,000. In addition, a right of private action is created whereby damages, attorney's fees, and other appropriate relief may be granted to any person with a kinship, cultural, tribal, research, scientific, or educational interest in preserving a site, the remains, or the associated goods. Failure to notify police of violations is punishable by a fine of from $100 to $500.

The act is administered by the Unmarked Burial Sites Preservation Review Board, which is chaired by the state archaeologist and is otherwise composed of a historian, four tribal representatives from the four resident Kansas tribes (the governing body of each tribe selecting one from its tribe), two "neutral" members from the general public, and a physical anthropologist employed by a state university. These individuals serve staggered terms of three years, and all receive compensation for their services, including expenses.

The board is responsible for maintaining a confidential register of all unmarked burial sites in the state and for administering the permitting process for excavations. Permits are issued only for scientific or educational purposes and only to bona fide research, medical, or educational institutions. The permit may only be valid for one year, though an extension of six months may be granted upon a showing of need. All remains and associated goods must be disposed of at the termination of the study as directed by the board and at the expense of the permittee. In the event the remains are identified as affiliated with a living tribe, that tribe may be consulted by the board for advice on appropriate disposition. In addition, a cemetery on state lands shall be established in which to inter remains and associated goods of individuals from unmarked burials for which other disposition of the remains has not been indicated by an affiliated tribe. The cemetery shall be closed to the general public.

The operative effect of the law will become clearer as regulations are implemented and a pattern of administration is established. In the interim, some questions arise. Does the state action in taking title to artifacts and in limiting the right of use of property until disposition of the remains is accomplished constitute a taking for which compensation must be paid to the property owner? What is intended by the reference to associated goods, recalling the issue in the California case of *People v Van Horn*? And is the statutory one-year limitation on study of the materials a sufficient period for full analysis?

Statutes

House Bill 2144 (1989 session), Kansas Unmarked Burial Sites Preservation Act.

Kentucky

Kentucky has no specific law relating to unmarked burials or to repatriation of grave goods. Neither does it have resident Indian tribal groups that have been recognized (Powell 1989:5). Rather, it applies its general health, cemetery, property, and criminal laws to prehistoric remains, as well as to contemporary and historic remains (Pollack 1989).

The Kentucky Archaeology Act (164.705, et seq.) applies only to land owned or controlled by the state and emphasizes preservation. Permits for excavation on state land are granted only to persons and educational institutions competent to add to the general store of knowledge concerning history, archaeology, and anthropology. Renewable permits are obtained from the Department of Anthropology at the University of Kentucky and expire each December 31. The Archaeology Act applies to artifacts, as well as to human remains.

A procedure employing the general state laws to permit archaeological excavation has developed. Upon the finding of human remains, the coroner is notified (72.020). The coroner then consults with the Justice Cabinet and the Vital Statistics section of the Department of Human Resources on the status of the context surrounding the remains. For archaeological analysis, application is made to the Vital Statistics section of the Department for Health Services for a permit to remove human remains (213.110). The permit contains an attestation by the applicant that the remains are antiquities and require preservation because of educational, cultural, or historical value. Following laboratory work, the

University of Kentucky Museum of Anthropology accepts the remains for curation (311.300–311.350).

The Museum of Anthropology has a written draft policy (version 2.1) whereby the museum is charged with treating all human remains with sensitivity and respect and will attempt to identify specific living Indian groups with affiliation to individuals whose remains are in its collection. Notification is sent to representatives of the appropriate groups with request for advice on proper manner of disposition of the remains, following scientific analysis. The museum will not publicly display any human skeletons except in specific educational exhibits on human biology and paleopathology. Cemetery laws apply to unmarked prehistoric burials, and unlike the law in many states, the mere fact that the land is no longer recognizable as a cemetery and that graves cannot be identified does not constitute abandonment of a cemetery (381.710). There is an additional interesting possibility under the state laws for protection of sites and grave goods. If a person dies without heirs or if the heirs neglect to claim their interest in the estate, all property passes by escheat to the state (393.020). If applicable to prehistoric grave goods, this might operate to convey ownership of all grave goods to the state and thus allow the state to protect aboriginal material even where it is contained in private property. Such a possibility has been considered by the office of the state attorney general in an informal opinion which suggests that there is no reason the state could not make this interpretation specific through statute (Goldman 1989).

Among other statutory provisions, enforcement of the laws is sought through application of 525.110, Desecration of Venerated Objects. It was through this provision that the defendants in the notorious Slack Farm looting incident (Arden 1989:376–92) were prosecuted (Powell 1989:3). Violation is a felony punished by incarceration in the state prison. The state laws are reported to work well in practice (Pollack 1989), but they are cumbersome. A task force has been formed to draft new legislation bringing all the applicable laws together. The new proposed legislation is scheduled to be presented to the state general assembly in 1990 (Powell 1989:11).

Statutes

Ky. Rev. Stat. Ann. 72.020, et seq., Bodies.
Ky. Rev. Stat. Ann. 164.705, et seq., Archaeology.
Ky. Rev. Stat. Ann. 213.110, Public Health.

Ky. Rev. Stat. Ann. 311.30, et seq., Occupations and Professions.
Ky. Rev. Stat. Ann. 381.710, et seq., Ownership and Conveyance of
Property.
Ky. Rev. Stat. Ann. 393.020, Property Subject to Escheat.
Ky. Rev. Stat. Ann. 512.020, Criminal Damage to Property.
Ky. Rev. Stat. Ann. 525.110, et seq., Desecration of Venerated Objects.
Ky. Rev. Stat. Ann. 514, et seq., Kentucky Penal Code.

Other Documents

University of Kentucky Museum of Anthropology Policy Statement,
draft version 2.1.

Louisiana

The Louisiana Archaeological Treasure Act (41:1601, et seq.) appears
to apply only to land owned by the state, and it is oriented toward
preservation of resources and not to repatriation of remains and grave
goods. The act creates the Louisiana Archaeological Survey and Antiquities Commission, which acts in an advisory capacity to the Department
of Culture. Indians are not specifically required on this commission,
though the Commission on Indian Affairs is to submit names of potential
candidates. The Archaeological Survey and Antiquities Commission is
charged with formulating reasonable rules and regulations to implement
the law as it applies to lands belonging to Louisiana (41:1607). The act
also establishes the office of the state archaeologist. It was amended in
1989 to clarify prior ambiguities (H.B. 1289; Act No. 291). All archaeological resources located in, on, or under the surface of lands belonging
to the state are declared to be the sole property of the state (41:1606).
Excavation is permitted only through contracts for salvage. Conversely,
sites and artifacts on private land are acknowledged to be the property of
the owner of the land and entitled to protection (41:1609; 1610). However, excavation on private land, especially excavation of Indian burial
sites, is strongly discouraged. Violations of the law are punished by a fine
of up to $500 and imprisonment for up to thirty days. Each day of
violation constitutes a separate offense. The act also establishes a civil

action to be brought by private citizens against violators, but this is only for temporary restraining orders and injunctions.

The state cemetery laws (8, et seq.) are extensive, and the definitions contained in the text are sufficiently broad to reasonably permit an interpretation that they apply to prehistoric aboriginal remains. If the cemetery laws do so apply, the penalties for disturbance of human remains (651, et seq.) are more severe than those imposed under the Archaeological Treasures Act. Potential fines are up to $5,000 and possible imprisonment is for up to one year.

The regulations implemented by the commission (Title 25), as discussed above, are interesting, especially subchapter G: Indian Burials (p. 25). There, the commission asserts that it is part of the state public policy that the cemetery law does apply to Indian burial sites (183), that there shall be no excavation on private land without a salvage contract from the state, and that all "burial furniture" recovered from all Indian sites is the property of the state unless direct heirs of the decedent make claim to the property. The Archaeological Treasure Act is cited as authority for this regulation. The state archaeologist advises that this language is overly broad, since grave goods found on private property remain the property of the landowner under Louisiana law (Byrd 1989b).

In September 1986, the state Division of Archaeology published a policy describing the competing values of scientific research and those representing the religious, spiritual, and philosophical significance of human remains. The policy expresses a preference for studying remains *in situ*, avoiding disrespectful displays of remains, and notifying genetic, ethnic, and cultural descendants of the decedent upon location of remains. Moreover, remains may be reinterred after study. Reportedly, Indian groups are considering new legislation (Byrd 1989a).

Statutes

House Bill No. 1289 (ACT No. 291), Amendment of La. Stat. Ch. 13, 41:1601, et seq. 1989.

La. Stat. Ann. 8, et seq., Cemeteries.

La. Stat. Ann. 41:1601, et seq., Archaeological Treasure.

Cases

Charrier v Bell, 496 So.2d 601 (La. Ct. App.), *cert. denied*, 498 So.2d 753 (La. 1986).

Other Documents

Division of Archaeology, Policy Statement on the Recovery, Analysis, and Reinterment of Human Remains Excavated at Archaeological Sites.
Louisiana Administrative Code Title 25, Cultural Resources, 1987.

Maine

The Maine Archaeological Heritage Act (371, et seq.) applies only to artifacts and only to land controlled by the state. In essence, it provides that all artifacts obtained from state-controlled lands or from voluntary donations are the property of the state and are to be turned over to the Maine State Museum for curation. The act also describes a permitting process for excavation on state lands, in which permits are issued by the director of the Maine Historic Preservation Commission. Violations of the act incur a penalty of $50 to $1,000.

Indian skeletal material is treated separately. The Indian Bones Law (4720) requires that, from October 3, 1973, onward, all Indian skeletal material, whether publicly or privately held, must be transferred to appropriate Indian tribes in Maine for reburial. Scientific study is allowed only by persons skilled in anthropology or archaeology, and then for no longer than one year from date of discovery. No penalty is stated for violations of the law. Despite its simplicity, the law is reported to work well in practice (Bradley 1989).

There are no statutory provisions for archaeological procedures. Those procedures that have evolved through practice are similarly simple. Upon discovery of aboriginal skeletal material, the state coroner and the state historical preservation officer or the State Museum are notified. Preference is given to preserve the remains *in situ*. If this is impossible, the remains are excavated and the Indian Bones Law is followed (Simon and Talmage 1989:5).

Part of the reason for the reported smooth operation of the laws is the paucity of well-preserved burials in Maine. In 1988 only three were reported, of which two were left in place and the third was removed due to erosion of the surrounding soil (Simon and Talmage 1989:5–6). Furthermore, there is healthy dialogue and cooperation between the Historic Preservation Commission, the State Museum, and the Maine

Indian tribes (Simon and Talmage 1989:5). The State Museum is currently analyzing the remainder of its skeletal material in preparation for return of the collection to the tribes.

Statutes

Me. Rev. Stat. Ann. 371, et seq., Archaeological Heritage.
Me. Rev. Stat. Ann. 4720, Indian Bones.

Maryland

The Maryland Archaeological Activities Act (2-301, et seq.) is oriented toward preservation and does not apply to private property. Excavation of archaeological resources on public land is the exclusive province of the state. Permits are issued to qualified institutions by the state Geological Survey of the State Historical Trust. Recovered items must be deposited for permanent preservation by a reputable institution. This appears to preclude repatriation and reburial of prehistoric aboriginal remains and grave goods. Violators incur penalties of up to $100 and imprisonment for up to thirty days. Similar provisions apply to archaeological resources discovered in caves (5-1404), except that the penalty is a fine of from $100 to $500 and imprisonment is from ten days to six months.

The general statutes prohibiting desecration of bodies (27-265) and graves (27-267) and providing permit procedures for disinterment of remains (4-251e) may also be applicable. Those who desecrate bodies may be imprisoned from five to fifteen years.

An active process is underway by the Council for Maryland Archaeology and the state Commission on Indian Affairs to present new legislation to the state legislature for greater protection of prehistoric remains and for the specific consideration of aboriginal sensitivities (Cole 1989). According to the council's Interim Burial Policy of July 1988, all human remains are to be treated with equal respect; affiliated ethnic, tribal, or family groups should be notified prior to excavation of any burial sites; if requested, reburial should be considered and laboratory analysis should not continue for longer than five years; if a burial is to be returned to any of the affiliated groups, return of associated grave goods will also be considered. A scientific review board, to be comprised of professional scientists and educators, is also proposed. The function of the board would be to review the scientific merit of all proposals for excavation. The policy as a basis for new legislation does not specifically apply to private property, though there is an implication that it might because it employs language referring to all archaeological excavations.

The present statutory regime does not offer much protection of pre-historic aboriginal remains and grave goods. Neither does it consider aboriginal sensitivities. However, the situation is in a state of flux and the final result will probably be more protective and sensitive, and it may well be a variation of the Interim Burial Policy of the Council for Maryland Archaeology.

Statutes

Md. Natural Resources Code Ann. 2-301, et seq., Archaeological Activities.

Md. Natural Resources Code Ann. 5-1401, et seq., Caves.

Md. Criminal Law Code Ann. 265, Removing Dead Bodies Without Permission.

Md. Criminal Law Code Ann. 267, Destroying, etc., Tombs, Trees, etc., in Cemeteries.

Md. General Health Code Ann. 4-215e, Permit for Disinterment.

Other Documents

Council for Maryland Archaeology: Interim Burial Policy, July 1988.

Massachusetts

The unmarked burial statutes (7:38, 9:26, 9:27c, 38:6b, 114:17) do not address the issue of disposition of grave goods. However, they do protect prehistoric aboriginal remains on both state and private lands. The laws protecting ancient human remains were enacted in 1983. Prior to this time, the Massachusetts laws did not protect unmarked graves

(Simon 1988:2). The Civil Rights Division of the attorney general's office declared the state cemetery laws unfair and discriminatory under the equal rights amendment of the state constitution, and the new laws were enacted, formalizing procedures previously put into place by the state archaeologist (Simon n.d.:1, 1988:3–4).

The Massachusetts Historical Commission Act (9:26–27) establishes the office of the state archaeologist and announces a policy favoring preservation of archaeological resources on land owned or controlled by the state rather than repatriation of them to aboriginal groups. Human remains are treated specifically and separately (9:27c). Anyone in the state who encounters remains suspected of being at least one hundred years old must cease all activity which might impair the integrity of the site until the state archaeologist has completed a site evaluation and made appropriate disposition of the remains.

Upon discovery of human remains, the county medical examiner is notified. If that officer finds the remains to exceed one hundred years of age, the state archaeologist is contacted, and if the remains are Indian, the Commission of Indian Affairs is also notified. This commission is the state agency charged with supervising matters concerning Indians in the state, and the law specifically gives it a role in the resolution of the disposition of the remains. The law does not assume scientific analysis will be conducted, and it contemplates several options for the disposition of the remains.

When an Indian site is investigated, the commission may supervise the effort. The commission and the state archaeologist consult with the landowner to determine if the site can reasonably be protected. If preservation *in situ* is impractical, an archaeologist will excavate the remains, which will then be analyzed by a qualified physical anthropologist. The analysis must be completed within one year unless an extension of time is granted by the state archaeologist and the commission. In practice, the remains are reburied in a protected location as close to the original burial site as possible (Simon 1988:5–6).

In addition to these laws, the general state laws now protect unmarked Indian cemeteries. Sites known or suspected to have contained the remains of one or more Indians continuously for a period of over one hundred years are included in the general cemeteries and burial statute (114:17; Bowman 1989:204). Violations of the cemetery laws are punished by a fine of from $100 to $500 and imprisonment for up to six months (114:43n).

The law is reported to work well in practice (Simon 1988:7, 10–11). From 1986 through 1988, the state archaeologist received notice of threats to twenty-nine sites. Seven required excavation and the remainder were preserved *in situ*. Local preservation required negotiation of terms with the property owners. The laws have helped improve relations with the Indian community, who now routinely report the presence and discovery of sites to the state archaeologist.

The act is relatively straightforward and appears to avoid many of the constitutional and other issues involved in the laws of other states. However, one lingering question involves the effect of the prohibition against use of the property until disposition is made of the remains. Does this constitute an interference with the commercial use of property that requires compensation to the property owner?

Statutes

Mass. Gen. Laws Ann. Ch. 7, Sect. 38A, Commission on Indian Affairs.
Mass. Gen. Laws Ann. Ch. 9, Sect. 26–27, Massachusetts Historical Commission.
Mass. Gen. Laws Ann. Ch. 114, Sect. 1, et seq., Cemeteries and Burials.
Mass. Gen. Laws Ann. Ch. 272, Sect. 71, et seq., Crimes Against Chastity, Morality, etc.

Michigan

The Michigan Aboriginal Records and Antiquities Act (299.51, et seq.) emphasizes preservation of archaeological resources and protection of the rights of private landowners. The statute defines "abandoned property" as including materials resulting from activities of historic and prehistoric Indians (291.51a), and further provides (299.54) that it is unlawful for any person to remove any relics or records of antiquity (specifically including human bones) from private property without the consent of the landowner.

A procedure has developed in the state for the treatment of prehistoric aboriginal remains and grave goods. Except for a planned archaeological excavation conducted by an established scientific institution, the local police agency is notified when prehistoric human remains are discovered. The police then notify the state archaeologist. If excavation and removal is desired, a permit is obtained from the local health department or by court order pursuant to the public health code (333.1, et seq.). The state archaeologist considers the sensitivities of affiliated clans and tribes. If the remains are on private land, the express permission of the landowner must also be obtained (750.160; Halsey 1986:1–2). However, prior to June 7, 1989, the statutory base for this procedure was unclear (Halsey 1989). The state attorney general issued an opinion on that date that clarifies the legal implications and confirms the propriety of the established procedure (Kelley 1989).

The opinion does not address whether or to what degree the general Cemetery or Burial Grounds Act (128.1, et seq.) applies to prehistoric aboriginal remains. However, the text of the statute is sufficiently broad to permit the application of these laws to prehistoric remains. Furthermore, the Penal Code (750.160), in attempting to protect the rights of property owners and scientific institutions, provides that disinterring or removing parts of any human body without legal authorization is guilty of a felony punishable by imprisonment for up to ten years and a fine of up to $5,000. Exceptions are granted for scientific acts conducted by established scientific institutions that have obtained the consent of the property owner. The statutes should then apply to disturbance of prehistoric human remains in all other circumstances. The relatively few discoveries of prehistoric aboriginal remains in the state may in part account for the recent resolution of the issue of applying general laws to them. In the past fifteen years, the only excavations have been in the context of salvage operations (Halsey 1989).

Statutes

Mich. Comp. Laws 128.1, et seq., Cemetery or Burial Grounds.
Mich. Comp. Laws 299.51, et seq., Aboriginal Records and Antiquities.
Mich. Comp. Laws 333.2853, et seq., Public Health Code.
Mich. Comp. Laws 750.160, Penal Code.

Minnesota

The Field Archaeology Statute (138.31, et seq.) establishes the Minnesota Historical Society, which is authorized to employ a state archaeologist. The society administers the statute with the assistance of the state archaeologist. The statute emphasizes preservation and does not contemplate repatriation of relics or artifacts to aboriginal claimants. It applies only to land owned, leased by, or subject to the paramount interest of the state.

The state and its licensees maintain exclusive right to excavate archaeological resources on state lands. The director of the society, with the approval of the state archaeologist, may issue licenses to qualified individuals to engage in archaeological excavations on specified state sites. The license may not exceed one year in duration, though extensions may be granted. The state retains title to all objects found and data gathered in the field. Violations constitute a gross misdemeanor and possible "blacklisting" of any involved institution from further licensing. It is the policy of the society to return skeletal remains to appropriate tribal people, to refuse to display aboriginal remains, and to cease collections of skeletal remains. In addition, the society has repatriated to appropriate Indian groups those items in the society's collections that are considered sacred by those groups (Disse 1987:2–3).

The Private Cemeteries Act (307.08) provides more specific protection of prehistoric aboriginal remains. It applies to all human remains and to both state and private lands. Any person who intentionally mutilates or removes human remains from a burial is guilty of a felony. Removal of artifacts from a burial is a gross misdemeanor. Burial sites may be posted by the state archaeologist for a distance of seventy-five feet around each burial ground. This statute applies to all unidentified human remains, other than those in platted or identified cemeteries, in a context that indicates antiquity greater than fifty years. Remains can be scientifically studied if the state archaeologist or the Indian Affairs Council (in the event the remains are Indian) deem such study to be advisable. If an affiliated tribe can be identified, the remains are turned over to the tribe for appropriate disposal. If remains discovered on private land are not removed, the property cannot be used in a manner that would disturb the remains. This has led to claims by property owners for compensation for interference with the right of use of the property affected (*Thompson, et al. v City of Red Wing*). To date, these claims have been unsuccessful in Minnesota.

Statutes

Minn. Stat. Ann. 138.31, et seq., Field Archaeology.
Minn. Stat. Ann. 307.08, Private Cemeteries.

Cases

Thompson, et al. v City of Red Wing, 455 N.W.2d 512 (Minn. App. 1990).

Mississippi

The state Antiquities Law (39-7-1, et seq.) has been in place since 1983. It applies to land owned or controlled by the state and to private property when the property owner has given specific consent to application of the law to the property. The stated public policy of the act is to locate, protect, and preserve archaeological sites. Excavation without permit and defacing of aboriginal markings or carvings is prohibited. Permits can be granted by the Board of Trustees who administer the Department of Archives and History. Violations incur fines of from $500 to $5,000 and imprisonment up to thirty days.

The state has no laws that specifically require consideration of aboriginal sensitivities or the possibility of repatriation of remains or artifacts to affiliated Indian groups. However, the general cemetery laws have been interpreted, applied, and enforced to protect prehistoric aboriginal graves and their contents, including associated grave goods (White 1980; anon. 1989c). Although there are several general laws that might have an impact upon the protection of prehistoric graves (McGahey n.d.:2–4), those with the greatest utility are the laws pertaining to Opening of Graves (97-29-23) and Desecration of Cemetery (97-29-25).

Any person who opens a grave for the purpose of moving human remains for sale or dissection, or of stealing grave goods, may be punished by a fine of up to $300 and imprisonment for up to two years. Any person who intentionally digs or in any way desecrates a cemetery is liable for a fine of up to $500 or imprisonment of up to one year. The definition of cemetery requires some form of discernible marking, although this may be through the use of natural objects such as trees. However, the requirement of discernible marking reduces the utility of this statute for the protection of ancient cemeteries where the markings have eroded. The office of the state attorney general has opined that excavations of archaeological landmarks under permit from the board of trustees are exceptions to the general application of the statutes (Pascoe 1978).

The statutes have been applied in cases of excavations on private land. Three men from Arkansas were convicted on January 4, 1989, of desecrating a prehistoric Indian site. They were imprisoned for thirty days and fined $1,000 each (anon. 1989c). The state is prepared to continue to apply these general statutes in the protection of its archaeological resources (McGahey n.d.:4).

Statutes

Miss. Code Ann. 39-7-1, et seq., Antiquities Law.
Miss. Code Ann. 97-29-23, Dead Bodies.
Miss. Code Ann. 97-29-25, Desecration of Cemetery.

Missouri

Missouri's cemetery laws were extended to private and abandoned cemeteries through the private cemetery law (214.131). Missouri's Unmarked Human Burial Sites Statute (194.400, et seq.) was passed in 1987 and affects both state and private land. It applies only to human remains and not to artifacts. The law specifically considers aboriginal sensitivities and ensures Indian participation in the decision-making process related to the disposition of human remains.

When any human remains—regardless of antiquity or ethnic identity—are discovered, the local police authority or the state historical preservation officer is to be notified. If there is no suggestion of criminal activity associated with the remains, the historical preservation officer takes jurisdiction and determines whether removal of the remains is required for their scientific analysis. An archaeological investigation must be made with a report within thirty days of the date of discovery of the remains, and under the statutory text, an investigation is stated to normally require excavation.

All ground-disturbing work that might affect the remains must cease within a radius of fifty feet of the site of suspected remains until disposition of them is made. This specifically includes commercial work on the property, but there is an unclear reference to the effect that a developer's efforts may not be delayed for more than thirty days. However, there is no provision for a procedure if the remains are still in place after the end of the thirty-day period. The state historic preservation officer attempts to identify the ethnic group with which the decedent was affiliated and solicits that group's advice on appropriate disposition of the remains.

Failing ethnic identification, the issue of disposition of the remains is referred to the Unmarked Human Burial Consultation Committee. The committee is composed of a cross-section of the state's population and includes Indian representatives. By a 1990 amendment (H.B. 1079), violations of the statute now constitute a class D felony punishable by up to five years' imprisonment and a fine of up to $10,000.

There are many problems with the statute. The potential issue of taking property without compensation arises again, and the statute also inadvertently imposes concurrent jurisdiction over contemporary human remains on the state historic preservation officer and the local county coroner through application of a pre-existing statute (205.630). Through its imprecise text, the statute also imposes potentially significant hardship on farmers, miners, developers, and other commercial users of property. In some areas in Missouri, fields have been worked for several generations and are permeated with minute bone fragments. According to the language of the law, these fields cannot be worked within a fifty-foot radius of any human material. This is one of several anomalous effects due to imprecise and ill-considered text.

Money is another major problem area with the law. Source of funding for the work required is not identified, and the law was presented to the state general assembly as entailing minimal cost (Di Pasquale n.d.). According to the principal framer of the bill, it was never anticipated that the state would pay for the work (Ellis 1988:1). Unfortunately, the cost burden was never assigned elsewhere and the state's taxpayers will bear the cost burden unless the law is modified. So far, in limited application of the law, much of the cost has been borne by developers concerned with undue delay to their projects (Israel 1989:1). The Missouri legislation is well intentioned, but poorly considered, and has many problems that will inevitably surface over time. Among other difficulties, there is no protection of artifacts. Perhaps precise implementing regulations and responsible administration of the confusing text will help remedy some of the defects. In the interim, a task force is now at work to develop amendments that address many of these deficiencies.

There is recent provision at law that offers some opportunity for relief. A new statute (S.B. 625) was passed and effective in September 1990. In essence, it provides that any native American group can establish a tribal or group burial ground or cemetery without the requirement that title pass first to the local county commission, as is the case for other cemeteries in the state. Penalty for desecration of newly established aboriginal burial sites is a class A misdemeanor that carries a fine of up to $1,000 per occurrence.

Statutes

Mo. Rev. Stat. 205.630, Coroners.

Mo. Rev. Stat. 214.131, Private Cemeteries.

Mo. Rev. Stat. 194.400, et seq., Unmarked Human Burial Sites. S.B. 625 (1990), Indian Burial Sites.

H.B. 1079 (1990), An Act to Repeal 413.265, 214.010, 214.040, 214.270, 214.310, 214.320, 214.330, 214.340, 214.350, 214.390, 214.410, RS Mo. 1986, and Sections 194.105 and 194.410, RS Mo. Supp. 1989, relating to death and certain funeral establishments and to enact in lieu thereof 19 new sections related to the same subject, with penalty provisions.

Montana

The state Antiquities Act (22-3-101, et seq.) pertains to preservation of archaeological resources on state land, with specific direction to the Montana Historical Society to collect Indian artifacts and implements. It does not apply to private property, except in cases where the property owner has given express permission. The Historical Preservation Office is also charged with drafting rules to guide other state agencies in the preservation of archaeological resources. Archaeological excavation on state land is the exclusive prerogative of the state. The historic preservation officer is authorized to grant permits to qualified institutions and individuals for the dissemination of knowledge. Objects collected remain the property of the state. Violations constitute a misdemeanor with fines of up to $1,000 and imprisonment for up to six months. Each day of violation constitutes a separate offense.

The state cemetery laws (35-21-701, et seq.) do not appear applicable to aboriginal prehistoric remains and grave goods, since the statutory text contemplates formal, marked places of interment. The health laws do appear applicable, as the Department of Health and Environmental Sciences is given broad authority over the disposition of human remains (50-1-101, et seq.). Because few prehistoric burials are encountered in Montana due to the lack of prehistoric aboriginal villages (Schwab 1989), however, these issues rarely arise.

Specific legislation (S.B. 434) was presented in 1989, but it failed in committee until questions about the constitutionality of some provisions could be studied and resolved. It will not be presented again until 1991. Draft rules for the treatment of prehistoric aboriginal remains and grave goods have been submitted by the Historical Society. Preference is given to *in situ* preservation, and display of human remains is prohibited. Display of sacred items should occur only in consultation with appropriate tribal groups, and the involvement of tribal authorities affiliated with aboriginal remains is strongly encouraged for all work with them, especially their ultimate disposition. These procedures also apply to associated grave goods. Although statutory treatment of the issues is ambiguous and proposed specific legislation has been postponed, the state Historical Society is given broad rule-making authority, and it has exercised this authority in drafting rules considerate of aboriginal sensitivities.

Statutes

Mont. Code Ann. 22-3-101, et seq., Antiquities.
Mont. Code Ann. 35-21-101, et seq., Mausoleum-Columbarium Act.
Mont. Code Ann. 50-1-101, et seq., Health and Safety.

Other Documents

Senate Bill 434, LC 0397/01, Cemetery Burial Sites and Human Remains Protection Act.

Nebraska

Nebraska passed an Unmarked Human Burial Sites and Skeletal Remains Protection Act (LB 340) in 1989. Prior to this statute, the state attorney general had characterized the state of the law in Nebraska pertaining to the disposition of aboriginal remains and grave goods as confusing, inconclusive, and lacking clear-cut legal authority on precise issues (Spire 1988:5). The new law is sweeping and applies to grave goods and human remains, and to private as well as to state property.

The statutory procedure contemplates scientific study and ultimate reburial. There are also provisions for limited repatriation of objects held in certain institutional collections. Human burial sites are to be left undisturbed to the maximum extent possible. When human remains or burial goods associated with an unmarked burial are encountered, ground-disturbing activities in the immediate vicinity of the location must cease until disposition of the remains and goods is made.

The police authorities are first contacted. The police officer then gives notice to the property owner, the county attorney, and the Nebraska State Historical Society. Assuming no criminal context, the society takes jurisdiction of the remains and attempts to ascertain the individual and tribal origin of the decedent. If the remains are not Indian and if there are no known relatives, the county coroner will arrange burial in the county cemetery, except that scientific study of the remains may be conducted for a period of one year at the option of the society. If the remains and associated grave goods are of extreme scientific importance, they may be curated until such time as they may be reinterred without impairing their scientific value.

If the remains and goods are of Indian origin, the state's Commission on Indian Affairs is notified, as well as known relatives or any tribes reasonably identified as affiliated with the decedent. Relatives or the tribe may reinter the decedent at their expense; otherwise the remains and grave goods will be buried by the county. Thus, all remains and associated goods of prehistoric Indians ultimately will be reburied. All institutions in the state that receive funding or formal recognition from the state and that hold Indian human remains and associated grave goods reasonably identified as affiliated with specific families or tribes must return these items to the family or tribe upon request. There is a statutory procedure for arbitration of disputed claims. These provisions do not apply to non-Indian remains.

Like the law in Idaho, the act also provides for enforcement through private civil action. Any person may bring a private action against individuals who have violated the law and may recover attorneys' fees and actual damages. Unlike Idaho's law, however, the statute does not specifically state that mental anguish is a compensable element of actual damages. Criminal prosecution is at the level of a misdemeanor.

There has not been sufficient time to observe the statute in action or for administrative rules to have been drafted. Thus, the full implications of the new law are yet to be appreciated. Some early questions arise. Is there a compensable interference by the state in the property owner's use of his property while awaiting resolution of the appropriate means of disposition of the remains and grave goods? Has the property owner been deprived of a right of ownership in the grave goods if there are no descendants with a paramount interest in them? Recalling the arguments raised in *People v Van Horn*, just what are associated burial goods under the statute? Does this include mortuary fill? And what is the implication of the federal constitutional requirements of equal protection of the special treatment accorded the repatriation of Indian remains, with the attendant arbitration procedure in the event of dispute, while maintaining silence on disputes pertaining to non-Indian remains?

Statutes

Legislative Bill 340, Unmarked Human Burial Sites and Skeletal Remains Protection Act, 1989.

Nevada

Nevada's new act relating to Indian burial sites (A.B.455) went into effect October 1, 1989. Rules have not yet been drafted for its administration, and because there is no operating history under it, the full extent of its effect cannot yet be assessed. The act modifies several existing statutes, and it was prompted apparently by incidents such as that at Overton, Nevada, in which commercial development of private land caused the destruction of known burial sites and multiroom dwellings of prehistoric Pueblos Indians (Hillinger 1988).

Under the existing Museums Law (381.195, et seq.), no excavation of any Indian site on state land is permissible without a permit issued by the director of the Division of Historic Preservation and Archaeology of the Department of Conservation and Natural Resources. The new act expands this to include Indian burials located on private land and dated from the middle of the eighteenth century until the commencement of the twentieth century, and it applies to any artifacts taken from such a burial site after October 1, 1989.

Anyone who discovers such a burial must report its location to the director of the Division of Historic Preservation; the division then consults immediately with the Nevada Indian Commission and the appropriate tribe. Archaeological excavation of the site may not be made without the consent of the tribe affiliated with the decedent. All artifacts and remains must be reinterred at the direction of the tribe and expense of the archaeologist. If there is no archaeological examination and the owner of the private property and the relevant tribe are unable to agree on a manner of interment of the remains, the landowner must reinter the remains and associated artifacts in a secure place and in a dignified manner, at the owner's expense.

The law prohibits sale or display of Indian remains and the possession of Indian artifacts taken from graves of the era described above. The act provides for civil action to be brought by an Indian tribe or an enrolled member of the tribe against violators. The civil plaintiff may obtain injunctive relief, attorney's fees, actual damages (including emotional distress), and punitive damages.

The state's Dead Bodies Statute (451.010, et seq.) may also be applicable, since the new act amends that statute to allow disinterment of Indian remains with authority of law. If so, that statute prohibits the opening of graves and removal of human remains and grave goods for the purpose of selling them or with malicious intent. Penalties include imprisonment for one to six years and a fine of up to $5,000.

The new act clearly considers the sensitivities of Indian tribes affiliated with remains. In pragmatic terms, it leaves untouched the treatment of prehistoric artifacts on private land and keeps the issue of prehistoric remains within the province of the Dead Bodies Statute. Issues remain regarding the possibility of compensation for interference with use of property and the confiscation of more recent artifacts. However, if the Dead Bodies Statute is applicable to these remains and artifacts in any event, such claims are not likely to be successful.

Statutes

Assembly Bill 455, An Act Relating to Indian Burial Sites, 29 April 1989.
Nev. Rev. Stat. Ann. 381.195, et seq., Preservation of Prehistoric and Historic Sites.
Nev. Rev. Stat. Ann. 452.020, et seq., Dead Bodies.

New Hampshire

The Historic Preservation Statute has been described as among the most comprehensive in New England (Simon and Talmage 1989:7). The office of the state attorney general has issued an opinion that as regards unmarked burials, the statute preempts application of the state's general Cemeteries Law (289:1, et seq.) and the state Burials and Disinterments Law (290:1, et seq.; Dunn 1988). The law is administered by the Division of Historical Resources through the state archaeologist. The division announces that its role is "nothing more than to speak for private cemeteries and Indian burial places which have no other advocate" (anon. n.d.:1).

The law applies to state and federal land and to prehistoric aboriginal remains and the grave goods associated with them. Except for human remains (by statutory definition these include associated grave goods), the state reserves to itself the ownership of all archaeological resources located on state land. Permits are issued to qualified individuals for archaeological excavations on state land. When any person discovers human remains, the county medical examiner is notified. If the remains are subject to the act, all ground-disturbing activities must cease until approval is given by the state archaeologist. If they are discovered by a professional archaeologist in the course of a field study, the remains may be retained for study for a period of up to four years. If remains are discovered on private property, the state archaeologist has forty-eight hours in which to make arrangements with the landowner for the protection or removal of the burial. Failing agreement within that period, the owner may resume ground-disturbing activities, apparently even with the destruction of the remains. If agreement with the property owner is achieved or the burial is on state land, and the remains are of Indian origin, the state archaeologist will notify affiliated Indian tribes or groups and solicit advice on the appropriate disposition of the remains, including the nature and extent of scientific analysis.

Priority for manner of disposition is given to wishes of the next of kin. If the remains are non-Indian and no close relatives are identified, the remains may be curated according to standard museum practices or reinterred in a public cemetery. The state Department of Transportation has transferred a parcel of land to the Division of Historical Resources to be used as a repository for the reburial of unmarked human remains (Potter 1989). Qualified institutions may also be given permission by the state archaeologist for long-term curation of remains discovered in the course of a professional excavation.

If remains are discovered during a professional excavation, the cost of transportation and reinterment of the remains is borne by the archaeologist or the sponsoring institution. If found on private land through noncommercial ground-disturbing activities, the Division of Historical Resources shall bear the cost. If discovered through commercial activities on private land, the owner or lessee of the property shall bear the cost. The law prohibits acquisition or sale of human remains (including associated grave goods) from unmarked burials after January 1, 1987, except as otherwise provided in the law for scientific and educational purposes. Violations constitute a misdemeanor, though discussions are now underway to elevate the crime to a felony (Simon and Talmage 1989:10).

The law is an intricate attempt to balance the interests of property owners, Indians, and the scientific and educational communities. It has seen little application in the two years of its existence. Only one discovery has been reported, and there has been no reported litigation under the law (Dunn 1989). The law has been successful, however, in encouraging developers to perform archaeological surveys prior to commencement of construction activities.

Statutes

N.H. Rev. Stat. Ann. 227-C:1, et seq., Historic Preservation.
N.H. Rev. Stat. Ann. 289:1, et seq., Cemeteries.
N.H. Rev. Stat. Ann. 290:1, et seq., Burials and Disinterments.

New Jersey

New Jersey has no laws that apply specifically to prehistoric aboriginal remains or grave goods. The Parks, Forestry and Recreation Statute (13:1B, et seq.) is oriented to preservation of archaeological resources on state land. There is no statutory base for repatriating or reburying items of aboriginal origin or sensitivity.

The degree to which the state general cemetery and burial laws (8A1:1-1) are applicable to prehistoric aboriginal remains is uncertain. The cemetery laws date generally to the late 1800s and contemplate European formal cemeteries and burials (Fimbel 1988:1). These laws address cemeteries and burials pertaining to religious organizations and are of doubtful relevance to prehistoric interments. One statute that might apply is the prohibition against desecration of venerated objects (2C:33-9). Venerated objects include burials and are not restricted to formal burials described in the general cemetery law.

In spite of the apparent lack of protection at law, respectful treatment of human remains is recognized by policies of the state agencies. The New Jersey State Museum immediately contacts Indian organizations upon the discovery of aboriginal remains and will not display skeletons or photographs of a sensitive nature (Fimbel 1988:1–2). Since at least 1984, the Office of New Jersey Heritage (the state historic preservation office) has followed draft guidelines which direct, *inter alia*, that all human remains will be accorded respectful treatment and that notice will be given to and advice sought from all interested parties, including groups who may be expected to have a generalized interest or affinity with the remains (McCarthy 1984). Thus, although there is no statutory protection for Indian sensitivities, practice in the state appears to recognize these sensitivities.

Few prehistoric burials are encountered within the state. Reportedly, there is little consensus among either the scientific community or the Indian community on the appropriate manner of dealing with prehistoric aboriginal remains or associated grave goods. Apparently, the Indian dissension is the result of a relatively small Indian population of approximately 10,000 individuals from at least nine distinct groups (Fimbel 1988:2–4). However, other reports suggest that Indian representatives are currently formulating a specific draft statute to present to the state legislature (Crazy Horse 1989).

Statutes

N.J. Stat. Ann. 2C:33-9, Desecration of Venerated Objects.
N.J. Stat. Ann. 8A:1-1, et seq., New Jersey Cemetery Act.
N.J. Stat. Ann. 13:1B, et seq., Parks, Forestry and Recreation.

New Mexico

In 1987 the office of the state attorney general issued an opinion suggesting that the state cemetery laws (58-17-1, et seq.) and laws against desecration of burials (30-12-12) did not apply to unmarked prehistoric interments (Mason 1987). In 1989 the state enacted a broad revision of its Cultural Properties Act (18-6-1, et seq.) and amended the Criminal Code to ensure that unmarked burials received protection at law.

The new act (H.B.57-1989) provides that any person who intentionally disturbs any human burial on state or private property, except under permit from the medical examiner or the Cultural Properties Review Committee, is guilty of a felony and subject to a fine of up to $5,000 and imprisonment for a term of eighteen months. A burial also includes associated grave goods. Any person who discovers a human burial must cease ground-disturbing activity and notify the local law enforcement agency. That office then notifies the medical examiner and the state historic preservation officer.

Applications can be made for excavation of the site. The Cultural Properties Review Committee will issue permits to qualified applicants who submit professional plans and provide for the reinterment of the remains and grave goods. Grave goods from sites on private property that are not required to be reinterred are the property of the landowner. It is also unlawful to excavate nonburial archaeological sites with earth-moving equipment on private land without first securing a permit from the committee. Recovered artifacts belong to the landowner, and the act does not prohibit the landowner from conducting personal excavations. Violations are punished by a fine of up to $1,000. Obviously, this law was designed to discourage commercial looting of sites. The Criminal Code was also amended to ensure that defacing marked prehistoric burials is deemed to be a criminal act.

The act does not appear to require consultation with affiliated aboriginal groups. However, the law contemplates regulations to be enacted for its administration, and these will probably include appropriate procedures. Since 1986, the state museum has followed the procedures described in its policy manual (anon. 1982, SRC rule 11). These procedures require consultation with affiliated cultural groups whenever sensitive cultural materials are dealt with, and the museum will consider return of such items to affiliated groups upon request. Again, practice and policies consider cultural sensitivities though the prior state law did not.

Statutes

House Bill 57, Act Relating to Burial Sites, 1989.
N.M. Stat. Ann. 18-6-1, et seq., Cultural Policies.
N.M. Stat. Ann. 30-12-12, et seq., Criminal Code.
N.M. Stat. Ann. 58-17-1, et seq., Endowed Care Cemetery Act.

New York

The state does not have a specific unmarked burial statute. However, as early as 1972 the New York Archaeological Council published a burial resolution that opposes excavation of burials for educational purposes, urges a moratorium on excavation of burials, supports reburial of remains in the manner prescribed by Indian representatives, suggests a joint Indian/archeological salvage effort for threatened sites, and requests the opportunity for scientific study of remains prior to reburial.

The Department of Historic Preservation (established under 14.01, et seq.) is attempting to implement a system whereby any activity that would disturb a designated burial site under the Indian Law (12-a) would require a permit from the Office of Parks, Recreation and Historic Preservation (Adams 1989a). These policies appear to have had tangible results even in the absence of direct statutory underpinnings. The New York State Museum is now contemplating voluntary repatriation of twelve culturally important wampum belts to the Onondaga Nation (Sobol 1989).

The state Indian cemetery law protects sites designated as places of historic interest, but not unmarked burials. Legislation and administrative regulations are being formulated to strengthen the law.

Statutes

N.Y. Education Law 233, State Museum, Collections.

N.Y. Education Law 234, Indian Collection.

N.Y. Parks, Recreation, and Historic Preservation Law 14.01, et seq., Historic Preservation.

N.Y. Indian Law 12-a, Indian Cemetery or Burial Grounds.

N.Y. Public Health Law 4216, Body Stealing.

N.Y. Public Health Law 4217, Receiving Stolen Body.

N.Y. Public Health Law 4218, Opening Graves.

Cases

Bailey v Miller, 143 NYS2d 122 (1955).

Other Documents

New York Archaeological Council Burial Resolution, 15 September, 1972; retyped January 1989.
New York Archaeological Council memorandum on Article 12-a and OPRHP proposed amendment and regulations, March 1989.

North Carolina

The state has an Indian population of approximately 65,000 and has had an unmarked burial statute (Gen. Stat. 70) in place since 1981 (Claggett 1988:1, 7). The law applies to all archaeological excavations on state land and to human burials on state and private land. It does not apply to grave goods on private land. Furthermore, the state statute against desecration of graves (14-149) applies to prehistoric unmarked burials. Violation of this act is a felony.

Any person with reasonable grounds to believe that human burials or remains are disturbed or exposed must contact the county medical examiner. Assuming the remains are Indian and there is no criminal context, the state chief archaeologist is notified. Ground-disturbing activities in the vicinity of the remains must cease, but in the case of private property this prohibition may not extend beyond forty-eight hours without the consent of the landowner.

If the remains are on state land or if the consent of the landowner has been obtained, and the remains are Indian, the chief archaeologist notifies the executive director of the North Carolina Commission of Indian Affairs. The director consults with the Eastern Band of Cherokee or other appropriate tribal group, and if possible, an agreement is reached that defines the type and duration of analysis to be performed on the remains and their ultimate disposition.

Reburial is not required when the executive director, with the advice of the appropriate tribal group, determines the manner of ultimate disposition. The landowner bears none of the cost of analysis or disposition of the remains. The affiliated tribal group may elect a site and mode of traditional disposition. If it decides not to do so, the executive director shall make the appropriate disposition, and the Commission of Indian Affairs shall bear the cost. Acquisition, sale, and retention of human remains from an unmarked burial after October 1, 1981, is a felony.

In the eight years the statute has been in existence, there has never been a reburial under it, even though the chief archaeologist and the Commission of Indian Affairs fully support the concept of reburial (Claggett 1989). The reported primary reason for this is ascribed to lack of substantive agreement within the Indian community about the appropriate disposition of the remains, the preferred location of that disposition, and which Indian community will bear the cost (Claggett 1988:3).

This is the reverse of the situation seen in states where there are operating policies considerate of Indian concerns even though there is no statutory protection. Here there is statutory protection and a willingness on the part of the administration to defer to Indian sensitivities, but the remains are left without traditional modes of respect nonetheless.

Statutes

N.C. Gen. Stat. 14-148, et seq., Criminal Trespass.
N.C. Gen. Stat. 70-1, et seq., Indian Antiquities, Archaeological Resources, and Unmarked Human Skeletal Remains Protection.

North Dakota

The year 1989 was a busy one for reburial legislation in the state. Five bills addressing the issue were presented to the state legislature: three failed (S.B. 2355, 2391, and 2466) and two passed (H.B. 1584 and S.B. 2372; Carvell 1989). The two successful bills greatly expand the scope of the state preservation laws. The preservation laws now apply to all archaeological excavations in the state and to grave goods as well as human remains.

The Burial Place and Resource Protection Act (307) provides that in the event human remains are discovered anywhere in the state, all ground-disturbing activity shall cease. Disturbance of a burial for monetary gain is a class B felony; otherwise it is a class C felony. Notification of the discovery must be given to the local law enforcement officer. Without authority of a permit issued by the superintendent of the state Historical Society, there can be no excavation of any archaeological resources on private or public land. Permits will only be granted to qualified individuals, and then only when the landowner agrees to deliver all human remains and associated grave goods to the superintendent.

The new Transfer of Historical Board Collection Items Act (682) gives the Historical Board established under the act broad discretion in determining disposal or transfer of items in its collection. Prior to the enactment of this law, the Historical Board was at court responding to an action that contested its decision to release all human skeletal remains and associated grave goods in its collection to appropriate tribal entities for reinterment on Indian lands (*Bratton v N. Dakota State Historical Board*). However, the new freedom given by the act may now make this action moot (Spaeth 1989).

The board has already enacted new rules with which to implement the increased discretion (40-01-03). All human remains and grave goods shall be released to the appropriate tribal entity for reinterment on tribal land. If the items were received by the board under conditions prohibiting such repatriation, the donor or owner of the items will be requested to give consent to the repatriation. If the consent is withheld, the Historical Society will so notify the intertribal reinterment committee and, upon request, provide the committee with the name and address of the party refusing consent.

The state legislature and the Historical Society have considered the priorities of competing values—those of educational and scientific advance and the integrity of private property on the one hand, and those of respectful treatment of human remains and proper consideration of Indian sensitivities on the other. The educational and scientific utility of retaining remains and grave goods in a museum collection was found wanting. However, questions still persist on the constitutional implications of the interference with the right to use private property.

Statutes

1989 N.D. Laws 307, Burial Place and Cultural Resource Protection.
1989 N.D. Laws 682, Transfer of Historical Board Collection Items.

Cases

Bratton v N. Dakota State Historical Board, unreported case, S.E. Jud. Dist. File No. 7853 (1989).

Other Documents

Chapter 40-01-03, North Dakota Administrative Code, Deaccession and Disposal of Collections, 1989.

Ohio

The Ohio Historical Society Act (149.30, et seq.) establishes the state Historical Society, the function of which is to identify and preserve state resources pertaining to Ohio history and archeology. The society is assisted by the Historic Site Preservation Advisory Board. One duty of the board is to suggest legislation necessary to the state's preservation program. There is no specific statutory provision for inclusion of aboriginal members on the board.

Under the Archaeological Landmarks Act (149.51, et seq.), the state Historical Society is to maintain a state registry of archaeological landmarks, including burials, and registered sites receive special protection. Sites located on private property cannot be placed in the registry without the permission of the landowner; otherwise, the statute applies only to sites on state land. The statute specifically provides that no skeletal material can be removed from a registered site without prior formal proceedings, including a permit. This may imply that skeletal material may be removed from sites not included in the register. Violations constitute a misdemeanor in the second degree.

The Ohio Administrative Code (149-1-02) states application procedures for excavation permits and details qualification requirements for entities and research proposals. There is no specific provision for consultation with affiliated aboriginal groups or for sensitive handling of sacred items. Proposed legislation (S.B. 244, LSB 118 0063-2, 1989–1990) is currently before the state legislature and is designed to strengthen the laws pertaining to treatment of human remains and to require consultation with affiliated ethnic groups on appropriate disposition of the remains. The new law applies to private property and also provides for Indian representation on a proposed Human Remains from Antiquity Board.

Some institutions have already implemented policies more considerate of aboriginal sensitivities than the present statutory law. The Cleveland Museum of Natural History has had in place since 1987 specific policies on the treatment of human remains and sacred items. In essence, the policies provide that human remains will be left in place unless they are threatened; that upon necessary disinterment members of groups affiliated with the remains will be notified; that there will be no reinterment without study and documentation; that human remains will not be accepted unless the alternative would result in inappropriate treatment of the remains; that there will be no public exhibition of the remains; that an advisory committee of "Native North Americans" is established to advise on treatment, disposition, and display of sacred items in the museum collection; and that consideration will be given to repatriation or possible loan to established tribal authorities of sacred items essential to the practice of traditional religion.

Protection of prehistoric aboriginal remains under the general laws is uncertain at best. The prohibition against abuse of a corpse (2927.01) makes such an act a felony. However, there have been Ohio court decisions that prehistoric Indian remains do not constitute a corpse for purposes of the general statutes (e.g. *State v Glass* and *Carter v City of Zanesville*). On the other hand, the prohibition against desecration (2927.11) specifically applies to Indian mounds and earthworks and to any site of great archaeological interest. However, violation of this section is only a misdemeanor.

Protection of prehistoric aboriginal remains and grave goods, and especially those located on private land, is a doubtful proposition under the present law. The proposed legislation, if successful, will improve this situation. In the interim, some comfort can be taken from enlightened voluntary policies such as those implemented by the Cleveland Museum of Natural History.

Statutes

Ohio Rev. Code Ann. 149.30, et seq., Ohio Historical Society.
Ohio Rev. Code Ann. 149.51, et seq., Archaeological Landmarks.
Ohio Rev. Code Ann. 2927.01, Abuse of a Corpse.
Ohio Rev. Code Ann. 2927.11, Desecration.

Cases

Carter v City of Zanesville, 52 NW 126 (Ohio 1898).
State v Glass, 273 NE2d 893 (Ohio App 1971).

Other Documents

S.B. #244, Historic Preservation. 1989–1990 session.
Ohio Administrative Code 149, et seq., Ohio Historical Society.
Policy Statement on Human Remains from Archaeological Contexts, Cleveland Museum of Natural History, March 1987.
Policy Statement on Native North American Sacred Objects, Cleveland Museum of Natural History, March 1987.

Oklahoma

Oklahoma has had an unmarked burial statute (21:1161–1168.6) since 1987. However, tribal groups have pressed for protection of remains and burial sites since the early 1970s, and they are a significant presence in the state, amounting to over 170,000 residents with seventy-three recognized tribal governments and several unrecognized tribal factions (Brooks 1988:5). In 1986 the office of the state attorney general offered an opinion (Turpen 1986) that described the procedures for legal excavation of archaeological sites, but that declined to opine on whether the state violation of sepulture laws (21:1151–1167) applied to prehistoric burials on the grounds that any such determination could only be made on a case-by-case basis.

The State Register of Historic Places Act (53:351, et seq.) applies only to burials on state land. The general statutes do not protect sites on private land for which the landowner has given consent to the excavation. Excavation of state land requires a permit issued by the state archaeologist, but penalties for violations are light. Fines are from $100 to $500, and imprisonment may be for a period of no more than thirty days.

More protection is offered by the state's unmarked burial statute. The law applies to both state and private property, and to grave goods as well as to human remains. Anyone who knowingly buys, sells, or barters for profit human skeletal remains or associated burial furniture is guilty of a felony, as is anyone who openly displays burial grounds, human remains, or burial furniture for profit. Institutions and museums are required to consult with leaders of tribes affiliated with the remains regarding scientific analysis of them and their ultimate disposition.

When remains or associated burial furniture are discovered, all ground-disturbing activity in the immediate vicinity must cease and the local police authority must be notified. If the remains are Indian, the state archaeologist must notify the leaders of tribes affiliated with the remains or grave goods, or the Oklahoma Indian Affairs Commission if no affiliated tribe can be located. The state historic preservation officer is notified in any event. To knowingly disturb human remains, burial furniture, or burial grounds without benefit of permit or other authority is a felony punishable by a fine of up to $1,000 and imprisonment for up to two years.

Questions arise as to the constitutional implications of interference with use of private property without compensation. This can more clearly be assessed with further experience under the law. At the moment, the statute is reported to be operating well. To the best knowledge of the office of the state attorney general, there is no pending litigation under the law (Mixon 1989). The substantial penalties imposed for violations are also reported to have discouraged pothunting in the state and may serve to "export" looters to neighboring states (Brooks 1988:10). Repatriation of remains and grave goods to Indian claimants is not specifically provided under the act, but this might be accomplished through regulations or mere operating policy on an ad hoc basis.

Statutes

Okla. Stat. Ann. 21:1151–1167, Violating Sepulture and Remains of the Dead.
Okla. Stat. Ann. 21:1161–1168.6, Reburial Law.
Okla. Stat. Ann. 53:351, et seq., Register of Historic Places Act.

Oregon

The Oregon statutes grant broad protection to Indian remains and grave goods whether located on state or private lands. The specific reburial statute (97.740, et seq.) essentially defines an Indian tribe as including any tribe recognized by the United States secretary of the interior. Seven tribes are recognized by the secretary, and three are also recognized by the state and therefore are covered by the statute (Gorospe 1985:41). The reburial statute applies to grave goods as well as to human remains and to private as well as to state lands. Under the reburial statute, no person may possess any Indian remains or artifacts taken from a cairn or grave after October 3, 1979, nor may anyone sell or display any such remains or artifacts. Violation of this provision is a felony. In addition, civil actions are provided for Indian tribes and their enrolled members that allow imputed damages of $500 or actual damages, whichever are greater, including damages for emotional stress. If the violation is willful, punitive damages may be awarded. Attorneys' fees may also be granted to a successful plaintiff.

The Archaeological Objects and Sites Act (358.905, et seq.) is a preservation statute that applies to state lands and to private property with the consent of the owner. All sales of archaeological objects in the state require a certificate of origin. All property, including money, used in any violation of the act may be confiscated by the state. Any archaeological objects seized become the property of the state and may be curated in the Oregon State Museum of Anthropology. Anyone who disturbs Indian remains must reinter those remains under the supervision of an Indian tribe. If a sacred item or an Indian-related site is discovered, the most appropriate Indian tribe must be notified and a representative of the tribe consulted on the ultimate repossession of any sacred items; any human remains would, of course, be dealt with under the reburial statute discussed above. Excavation of archaeological sites may take place on state lands only under authorization of a permit issued by the Division of State Lands in consultation with the state Historic Preservation Office (273.705). This is confirmed by the office of the state attorney general (Arnold 1988:4). Under this statute, an archaeological site does not encompass human remains and only applies to objects at least seventy-five years old. The statutes are reported to work well in practice (Ross 1988:140). However, the old question regarding interference with the use of private property persists.

Statutes

Or. Rev. Stat. 97.740, et seq., Protection of Indian Graves.
Or. Rev. Stat. 273.705, et seq., Removal of Historical and Other Valuable Materials.
Or. Rev. Stat. 358.905, et seq., Archaeological Objects and Sites.

Pennsylvania

The state History Code (37:101, et seq.) asserts a policy of preserving remains, objects, and evidence of prehistoric or anthropological value. The emphasis is on conservation, research, restoration, and storage of archaeological resources. This policy is administered by the state Historical and Museum Commission of the Commonwealth. This commission appoints the Historic Preservation Board, which administers the state Historic Preservation Act (37:501, et seq.). This act has a similar orientation and applies only to state lands. Excavation of archaeological resources on state lands is the exclusive province of the state, except under authority of a permit. Violators incur fines of up to $2,500 and imprisonment for up to one year.

The general statutes against desecration of burials (18:5509) and abuse of corpses (18:5510) offer some protection to unmarked burials. Violations are misdemeanors in the second degree and carry prison sentences of up to two years. In addition, under authority of the state removal of remains law (9:51, 52), plea can be made at court for removal of remains from private burial grounds when the grounds become unsuitable due to activity such as development. This recourse has largely been employed by archaeologists in salvage efforts (Roberts 1984:237). However, it might also be employed by Indians who wish to secure the remains of decedents with whom they have tribal or lineal affinity.

The state Historical and Museum Commission has published a policy on the treatment of human remains (Raber 1985:161–62) that calls for respectful treatment of all remains, responsible scientific analysis of remains, excavation to be conducted only when necessary and scientifically desirable, no public display of remains, and no reburial of remains in a manner inconsistent with the beliefs of the ethnic group associated with them. Reburial is not otherwise addressed. There is no reference to repatriation of grave goods, and there is no specific provision for Indian participation in the decision-making process regarding appropriate disposition of aboriginal remains. However, as revealed by a questionnaire distributed to the members of the state Archaeological Council, the professional community in the state is highly aware of the issues and interested in addressing aboriginal concerns (Neusius 1989).

Statutes

Pa. Stat. Ann. 9:51, 52, Removal of Remains.
Pa. Cons. Stat. 18:5509, Desecration of Venerated Objects.
Pa. Cons. Stat. 18:5510, Abuse of Corpse.
Pa. Cons. Stat. 37:101, et seq., History Code.
Pa. Cons. Stat. 37:501, et seq., Historic Preservation Act.

Rhode Island

The state Antiquities Act (42-45.1-1, et seq.) requires the state Historical Preservation Commission to identify, interpret, preserve, and protect archaeological resources, including burials. This appears to present an obstacle to repatriation or reburial of prehistoric aboriginal remains and grave goods. The general statutes offer some protection in that the desecration of graves statute (11-44-31) applies to "any . . . facility used for the purpose of burial." Violators incur a fine of up to $5,000 and imprisonment for up to three years. On the other hand, the cemeteries statute (23-18-1) contains narrow, formal definitions and does not appear applicable to traditional aboriginal cemeteries.

Current reburial policies in the state remain vague and are negotiated on a case-by-case basis. A plea has been made for discussions by involved groups to air their concerns and structure a mutually satisfactory solution (Morenon 1987:5–6).

Simon and Talmage (1989:8) describe the operating procedures in the state. At the moment, when skeletal remains are discovered, the police and the medical examiner are notified. If the remains are Indian, the state archaeologist is notified. The state archaeologist then contacts the Narragansett tribal officials for informal consultation on the treatment of the remains. The Historic Preservation Commission also has broad guidelines, applicable to all archaeological site investigations, that recommend coordination of activities with the Narragansett tribe. However, reported factionalization within the tribe is said to make negotiated agreements difficult.

Statutes

R.I. Gen. Laws 11-44-31, Desecration of Places of Public Assemblage.
R.I. Gen. Laws 23-18-1, Cemeteries.
R.I. Gen. Laws 42-45.1-1, et seq., Antiquities Act.

South Carolina

The state Underwater Antiquities legislation (54-7-400, et seq.) is oriented toward preservation. The act is administered through the Institute of Archaeology and Anthropology (60-13-01, et seq.), whose director is the state archaeologist. The institute is a part of the University of South Carolina. There is no equivalent legislation for land sites (Ashworth 1987). Objects discovered under state waters are the property of the state and are held by the institute. There is also statutory provision for a state museum (60-13-30).

There are no statutes directly applicable to prehistoric aboriginal remains or grave goods (Rathbun 1989). However, the text of the general statute prohibiting desecration of graves (16-17-600) is sufficiently broad to apply to prehistoric remains, though this application is not definitely resolved. The penalties would include a fine of up to $2,000 and imprisonment for up to five years.

Informal policies have developed within the state whereby, upon discovery of ancient remains, local coroners contact either the forensic anthropologist at the University of South Carolina or the state archaeologist for advice and suggestions. Similarly, the state Highway Department is reported to be especially sensitive to treatment of prehistoric remains (Rathbun 1989). A specific law similar to that in Oklahoma for the protection of cemeteries, abandoned cemeteries, human burials, and human skeletal remains is reported to have been offered to the state legislature in November 1987, but there has been no further action on the draft.

To the best of the author's knowledge, state legislation and policies do not consider Indian sensitivities. There is no contemplation of repatriation of remains or artifacts, and there is no indication of involvement of Indian representatives in decisions pertaining to proper disposition of prehistoric Indian remains.

Statutes

S.C. Code Ann. 16-17-600, Destruction of Graves and Graveyards.
S.C. Code Ann. 54-7-400, et seq., South Carolina Underwater Antiquities Act.
S.C. Code Ann. 60-13-01, et seq., Antiquities Act.

Other Documents

Proposed Law for the Protection of Cemeteries, Abandoned Cemeteries, Human Burials and Skeletal Remains, Nov. 1987.

South Dakota

The Archaeological Exploration Act (1-20-17, et seq.) addresses concerns of preservation and specifically applies to mounds and burials, as well as to relics and artifacts. The act applies only to state lands and is administered by the state archaeologist. Reburial and repatriation of archaeological resources is not specifically contemplated by the statute. Archaeological excavation on state lands is the exclusive province of the state. Permits may be issued to qualified institutions. Materials collected under permit are the permanent property of the state, and the state archaeologist is obliged to arrange for disposition of the items in an appropriate institution of the state or to loan the items to qualified institutions in or out of the state. Unauthorized excavation by others constitutes a class 2 misdemeanor.

The general state laws may afford protection to prehistoric aboriginal remains. The desecration of graves statute (34-27-18) prohibits intentional removal of bodies from graves or coffins, and the coroners statute (34-26-14) gives the coroner custody of remains until there is opportunity for investigation or inquest. Removal of bodies and associated grave goods is punishable by a fine of up to $1,000 and imprisonment for up to one year. The Administrative Rules of the state describe a procedure to be followed when human remains are discovered in an unmarked grave on state lands (24:52:04 1986). Ground-disturbing activity must cease and the state archaeologist must be notified within forty-eight hours of the discovery. Assuming there is no criminal factor involving the remains, the state archaeologist takes custody of them and effects their scientific analysis at state expense. If tribal identity can be established, the remains may be released to appropriately affiliated groups. Reinterment of remains occurs within five years of discovery unless the state archaeologist determines that they are of extreme scientific importance.

In 1986 a huge reburial effort took place that involved hundreds of Indian skeletons previously held in the collection of the Archaeological Research Center at Fort Meade. The reburial followed years of intense study of the remains, and it was conducted under the supervision of Arikara tribe elders. This disposed of the major portion of the contentious skeletal materials held in the state's collections (Alex 1986:5–6). The state Historical Society reports that no reburials involving state funds have occurred since that effort (Keller 1989).

Statutes

S.D. Codified Laws Ann. 1-20-17, et seq., Archaeological Exploration.
S.D. Codified Laws Ann. 34-26-14, Right to Custody of Dead Body.
S.D. Codified Laws Ann. 34-27-18, Opening Grave, etc.

Other Documents

Administrative Rules of South Dakota 24:52:04, Discovery and Reburial of Human Remains, 16 September 1986.

Tennessee

The state's Archaeology Law (11-6-101, et seq.) applies only to state lands and not to private property, except that it is a misdemeanor to excavate on private property without the consent of the owner. The Division of Archaeology controls all archaeological efforts, and permits are issued by the state archaeologist. All resources recovered are the property of the state and must be used solely for scientific or public educational purposes. This would seem to preclude repatriation or reburial of sensitive aboriginal materials.

The state's general statutes offer broader protection. The desecration of graves statute (39-3-1327) applies to unmarked prehistoric interments. Violations are felonies and lead to fines of $3,000 and imprisonment of from one to five years. Cemetery destruction (39-6-701) is also a criminal act.

The statute on abandoned cemeteries (46-6-101) applies to prehistoric cemeteries and allows removal of cemeteries pursuant to court order and under conditions acceptable to the relatives of the decedents. This is often employed in the context of highway or subdivision construction, and special rules have been developed for use with traditional Indian cemeteries (Fielder 1989:3). These rules, as of January 1989, do not specifically entail consultation with affiliated tribes. However, reburial must take place, following scientific analysis. There is no reference to grave goods.

Although the statutes offer broad protection to burials, application of the general cemetery and burial laws to prehistoric sites has drawn some complaint. Court-ordered removal of human remains under cemetery laws does not necessarily contemplate preservation of the archaeological record, especially in the context of real estate development. Thus, much archaeological data associated with remains is often lost (Moore 1989:11).

Statutory protection of aboriginal remains attempts to treat these remains with the same respect shown all decedents (Fielder 1989:3). However, there is no apparent special consideration for Indian sensitivities regarding remains or grave goods. Presumably, grave goods are reinterred with the remains just as with contemporary burials.

Statutes

Tenn. Code Ann. 11-6-101, et seq., Archaeology.
Tenn. Code Ann. 39-3-1327, Vandalism of Houses of Worship, Graveyards, Cemeteries, etc.
Tenn. Code Ann. 39-6-701, et seq., Cemeteries.
Tenn. Code Ann. 46-4-101, et seq., Termination of Use of Land as Cemetery.

Texas

The Texas Antiquities Act (191.001, et seq.) applies only to land owned or controlled by the state. The law emphasizes preservation and establishes the state Antiquities Committee as the custodian of all materials found on state land. Although it does not specifically refer to burials, it does refer to all archaeological sites. All archaeological resources recovered from state land are the exclusive property of the state, though the Antiquities Committee may issue excavation permits. Repatriation and reburial are not dealt with by the statute. Violations are punishable by fines of from $50 to $1,000 and imprisonment up to thirty days. Each day of violation is a separate offense.

In Texas, private lands account for over 90 percent of the state. Allegedly, a thriving and probably legal network of commercial pothunters has developed that targets unmarked Indian and early historic graves (Mercado-Allinger 1989). A bill (H.B.2434/S.B.1327) designed to offer some protection to remains on private property was introduced in the 1989 Texas Legislature, but it was not successful. This was the second attempt by the Texas Historical Commission to introduce legislation to remedy the problem.

There are general statutes, but their applicability to prehistoric aboriginal interments is doubtful. The office of the state attorney general was asked by the Historical Commission to opine whether these laws were applicable. In response, that office described laws that might be applicable (for example, stealing from a corpse [31.03]; desecration of a venerated object [42.09]; abuse of a corpse [42.10]) but declined to give a general response on the basis that the element of the requisite intent to commit a crime had to be assessed on a case-by-case basis (Davis 1989). Clearly, the statutory regime does not give priority to aboriginal sensitivities. Repatriation and reburial of remains are not contemplated since the laws favor other values, such as private ownership of land and the subterranean contents thereof.

Statutes

Tex. Code Ann. 31.03, Penal Code.
Tex. Code Ann. 42.09, Penal Code.
Tex. Code Ann. 42.10, Penal Code.
Tex. Code Ann. 191.001, et seq., Natural Resources Code.

Utah

The Utah Antiquities Act (63-18-1, et seq.) applies only to state lands and is a preservation statute. It does not apply to private property, except with the consent of the landowner. Excavation of archaeological resources is the exclusive province of the state, but permits may be issued by the Division of State History. The law specifically requires that a maximum amount of archaeological information must be recovered and preserved, in addition to the physical recovery of items. This appears to preclude repatriation or reburial of remains or grave goods. There is no provision for notification of or consultation with aboriginal representatives upon discovery of aboriginal burials. Violation of the act is a misdemeanor. Proposed revisions to the law are now being written and will be submitted to the state legislature in 1990 (Christensen 1989).

The statute prohibiting desecration of bodies (76-9-704) was amended in 1988 and applies to unmarked prehistoric burials. If an individual disturbs a dead human body, the consequent crime is a third degree felony. Failure to report the discovery of a body is a class A misdemeanor. Archaeological excavation pursuant to the Antiquities Act is excepted from this law. The law applies to private property, but it has yet to be tested in court in the context of prehistoric aboriginal burials (Christensen 1989).

The statutory structure is not sensitive to aboriginal concerns regarding disposition of remains and grave goods. However, administrative policy for discoveries on state land may be more responsive. The policy of the Society for American Archaeology encourages close cooperation between scholars engaged in the study of human remains and the communities that may have biological or cultural affinity to those remains. The Division of State History subscribes to that policy (Madsen 1989).

Statutes

Utah Code Ann. 63-18-1, et seq., Division of State History.
Utah Code Ann. 76-9-704, Abuse or Desecration of a Dead Human Body.

Vermont

Vermont does not have laws or regulations dealing specifically with unmarked burials or grave goods. The general statute for removal of bodies (18:5212) prescribes a permit from the town clerk. Violations carry a penalty of up to $1,000 and five years' imprisonment. The general cemetery law (18:5302) may also be applicable, as it pertains to any plot of ground for the burial or disposition in a grave of the remains of human dead.

The state Historic Preservation Law (22:14-701, et seq.) espouses preservation and applies only to state lands. It specifically contemplates aboriginal mounds and burial sites. All archaeological resources on state lands are declared the property of the state. Excavation by others is prohibited, except under authority of a permit issued by the director of the Division for Historic Preservation with the advice of the state archaeologist. There is no statutory provision for repatriation or reburial of prehistoric remains or grave goods, or for aboriginal participation in decisions relating to disposition of remains affiliated with specific tribes. Violators may be fined up to $1,000 and imprisoned up to six months.

In 1988 a major test of the state's general laws to protect prehistoric aboriginal remains arose in *State v DuBois and LaRocque*. In this case, property developers encountered a prehistoric traditional Abenaki cemetery. The state obtained a temporary restraining order enjoining further development based on application of the general laws described above. The case was ultimately resolved through the purchase of the property by the Vermont Nature Conservancy (Yudien 1989), but the action did establish the utility of the general statutes to help preserve prehistoric aboriginal sites.

Simon and Talmage report that there are no reliable statistics on the number of unmarked burials encountered in the state because there is no legal duty to report them (1989:9). The state's Department of Historic Preservation is developing guidelines for the treatment of human remains and is studying possible amendment of the state cemetery laws.

Statutes

Vt. Stat. Ann. 18:5212, Permit to Remove Dead Bodies.
Vt. Stat. Ann. 18:5302, Cemeteries.
Vt. Stat. Ann. 22:14-701, et seq., Historic Preservation.

Cases

State of Vermont v DuBois and LaRocque, unreported case, Vt. Superior Court Docket No. S-155-88Fc, 1988.

Virginia

The Virginia Antiquities Act (H.B. 1748) was passed in 1989, and operating regulations will not be available for approximately eighteen months (Slusher 1989). Accordingly, the implications of the new law remain uncertain. In general, the act applies only to state lands and is administered through the newly created Department of Historic Resources. Portions of the act are similar to the laws of Utah in that collection and preservation of archaeological resources is required to the maximum extent possible. An exception arises with the discovery of human remains.

No archaeological excavation of human remains anywhere in the state may be undertaken without a permit issued by the director of the Department of Historic Resources. Furthermore, the department is declared to be an interested party in court proceedings dealing with abandonment of cemeteries. Decisions of the director may be appealed to the local circuit court. Violations are a class 1 misdemeanor. No provision is made regarding grave goods, or the repatriation or reburial of items discovered, except that the eventual regulations are to address procedures for the ultimate disposition of human remains.

The general cemetery and desecration laws apply to prehistoric aboriginal remains. The Crimes and Offenses Statute (18.2-125, et seq.) prohibits disinterring bodies from a burial place and tampering with tombs and markers. Violation is a class 4 felony punishable by imprisonment for a period of two to four years. The Religious and Charitable Matters Statute (57-35.1, et seq.) provides methods for removal of bodies from abandoned cemeteries. Before the enactment of the Antiquities Act, permission for archaeological excavation was obtained through the local circuit court. This sometimes produced conflicting results within the state, including occasions in which immediate reburial without scientific analysis was required. The new act is designed to assure consistency in the permitting process and in the retrieval of archaeological data.

Human remains are now protected in the state, but consideration of aboriginal sensitivities and participation of aborigines in decision making is lacking. The state laws mandate data retrieval and preservation and do not contemplate repatriation or reburial of items unearthed. Eventual regulations may mitigate this situation, but it is difficult to envision such procedures given the statutory emphasis on preservation.

Statutes

Va. Code Ann. 10.1-2300, et seq., Virginia Antiquities Act.
Va. Code Ann. 18.2-125, et seq., Crimes and Offenses.
Va. Code Ann. 57-35.1, et seq., Religious and Charitable Matters.

Washington

The state Archaeology and Historic Preservation Act (27.34) establishes the state Heritage Council, which is charged with adopting a statewide plan for archaeology, among other things. The act also establishes the Office of Archaeology and Historic Preservation (this office is a part of the Department of Community Development), which is to be administered by the state preservation officer. This essentially is a preservation law and provides for a state registry of significant sites.

Effective July 23, 1989, the new act pertaining to archaeological objects and sites (S.B. 5807) amends the prior law as presented in the Archaeological Sites and Resources Act (27.53) and the Indian Graves and Records Act (27.44). The act provides that all archaeological sites and material in the state are resources of the state. Excavation without a permit from the director of community development is prohibited. Although no one, including the landowner, may excavate on private property without a permit, the director is not allowed to issue a permit for excavation on private property without the prior permission of the landowner. Guidelines for issuance of permits must be developed in consultation with representatives of Indian tribes.

The Indian Graves and Records Act (27.44), as amended by the new law, prohibits any disturbance of a cairn or grave of a native Indian, and this prohibition is not restricted to public land. Violation constitutes a felony. Archaeological examination is permitted of graves and cairns, but only with ultimate reinterment or responsible curation and with the permission of the state historical preservation officer, who must first notify any tribes affiliated with the decedent. Any intentional disturbance of an aboriginal burial is a felony. In the event of an inadvertent disturbance, the individuals responsible must reinter the remains under the supervision of the appropriate tribe and at the expense of the Office of Archaeology and Historic Property. The act also prohibits the sale of Indian grave goods.

The possibility of civil action is established on behalf of tribal members against violators of the act. The minimum damages are $500 or actual damages, whichever are greater, plus attorneys' fees. Punitive damages may also be awarded upon proof of intentional disturbance, and this award is paid to the Office of Archaeology and Historic Preservation.

The state Administrative Code (WAC 25-48) sets out the permitting procedure under these acts. There is to be no removal of material from an Indian cairn or grave, except by authority of a permit issued by the Office of Archaeology and Historic Preservation. Except in the case of emergency salvage efforts, affected Indian tribes must be given at least thirty days' notice prior to issuance of a permit and then must be notified upon issuance of the permit. The permit may include conditions requested by the affected Indian tribe.

Some general state statutes also appear applicable. The desecration statutes (68.50.140–.150) prohibit removal and disturbance of dead bodies without authority of law, including material associated with those bodies. Penalties can include fines of up to $1,000 and imprisonment for up to five years. The new law offers broad protection of traditional aboriginal burials and grave goods, and it calls for considerable Indian participation in the various processes. The question remains whether the extension of this protection to private property raises issues of taking property without compensation.

Statutes

Senate Bill 5807, Act Relating to Archaeological Objects and Sites, 23 July 1989.
Wash. Rev. Code Ann. 27.34, Archaeology and Historic Preservation.
Wash. Rev. Code Ann. 27.44, Indian Graves and Records.
Wash. Rev. Code Ann. 27.53, Archaeological Sites and Resources.
Wash. Rev. Code Ann. 68.50.140–.150, Desecration of Remains.

Other Documents

Wash. Admin. Code 25-48, Archaeological Excavation Permit.

West Virginia

The state Historic Landmarks Commission is required to identify, study, and preserve archaeological sites on public lands (8-26A-1, et seq.). Municipalities and county governments are also allowed to establish similar local commissions. No ground-disturbing activity is permitted around earthworks of archaeological importance unless a certificate of appropriation has first been issued to regulate the activity around the sensitive site. Violators incur a fine of up to $500 and imprisonment for up to six months.

The Department of Culture and History establishes the Archives and History Commission (29-1-5, et seq.). This commission is to be comprised of nine individuals representing the cultural and ethnic identity of the state. Thus, if properly constituted, it could provide a forum for aboriginal participation in decision-making processes. One duty of the commission is to approve rules required to be established by the director of the Division of Archives and History regarding permitting processes for archaeological excavation on state lands. Otherwise, there is no reference to repatriation, reburial, or aboriginal participation in any process.

The general cemetery laws (35-5-1) do not appear helpful for the protection of prehistoric aboriginal remains—the text employed is directed toward formal, dedicated cemeteries. However, other laws may be useful. Upon court order, remains can be transferred from private interments on private land (37-13-1, et seq.). If the owner of the property were sympathetic and cooperative, Indians might be able to employ this statute to secure the removal of known aboriginal remains from private property and reinter them in secure locations with appropriate ceremony. Moreover, the prohibition against desecration of dead bodies (61-8-14) appears broad enough to apply to prehistoric aboriginal remains. The penalty for violation is imprisonment for a period of from two to five years.

The state preservation laws are relatively narrow in application, and the general laws carry problems in the definitions of "grave" and "ceme-

tery." These deficiencies and others are noted by the West Virginia
Native American Committee (Karus 1989) and the state Department of
Culture and History (Bloemker [1989]). Each of these entities is studying
possible strengthening of the state's laws.

Statutes

W.V. Code 8-26A-1, et seq., Historic Landmarks Commission.
W.V. Code 29-1-5, et seq., Department of Culture and History.
W.V. Code 35-5-1, et seq., Cemeteries.
W.V. Code 37-13-1, et seq., Removal, Transfer, and Disposition of
    Remains in Graves Located Upon Privately Owned Lands.
W.V. Code 61-8-14, Disinterment or Displacement of Dead Body or Part
    Thereof.

Wisconsin

In 1987 the state enacted legislation granting broad and equal protection to all burials located within the state. The Disposition of Human
Remains Statute (157) was expanded (at 157.70, et seq.) to apply to
unmarked burials and their contents. The law applies to private and
public lands, and to burial goods as well as human remains, and it
specifically contemplates aboriginal participation and notification in the
decision-making processes. The act is administered by the director of the
state Historical Society.

The law establishes two categories of sites, those that are catalogued
by the director and those that are not. All discoveries on public lands are
considered to be catalogued sites. The director is required to maintain a
catalogue of identified sites with an accompanying registry of individuals
whom the Burial Site Preservation Board determines to have a substantial interest in the site. As of April 1988, approximately 4,840 European-
American sites and 835 "archaeological" sites had been recorded (Riggs
1988:7). The board is comprised of the state archaeologist, the state
historical preservation officer, the director of the state Historical Society,
three professional scientists, and three members of federally recognized
Indian tribes or bands.

In addition to identifying individuals with an interest in sites, the board also reviews determinations of the director and approves transfers of burial sites on public land. Specific statutory duties of the director include maintaining a toll-free telephone service for reporting the discovery or disturbance of sites, assisting Indian tribes in negotiating with federal agencies for preservation of burial sites, and mediating disputes between landowners and others concerning the disturbance of sites.

The law prohibits any disturbance of a burial site, except under permit issued by the director. When a human burial is discovered at an uncatalogued site, ground-disturbing activities must cease. The director determines if any individuals listed on the registry may have a substantial interest in the site. If so, those individuals are given notice of the discovery, and the landowner may either alter the activity so as not to disturb the burial or give permission to the director to remove and analyze the remains. At catalogued sites, an application for a permit to disturb the site is filed.

The director must notify the individuals on the registry and make a determination of the advantages of the application by giving weight to the following interests (listed in order of priority): direct kinship; cultural, tribal, or religious affiliation; scientific, educational, or environmental objectives; commercial purposes unrelated to land use; any other interest deemed by the board to be in the public interest. Following analysis, the remains will be disposed of according to the wishes of individuals listed on the registry, with priority given first to those having kinship or cultural affiliation and then to those having tribal or religious affiliation. If none of the notified parties applies for specific disposition of the remains, they will be reinterred or curated at the discretion of the director, subject to the review of the board (draft H.S. 2.07 [6]-[9]).

Violators can incur fines of up to $5,000 and imprisonment for up to one year. In addition, a civil action is established on behalf of individuals interested in the preservation of the site or reinterment of the remains and associated items. Actual damages and attorney's fees can be awarded to a successful plaintiff. To date, the office of the state attorney general is unaware of any actions at law involving this statute (Wilker 1989).

Statutes

Wis. Stat. Ann. 157.01, et seq., Disposition of Human Remains.

Other Documents

H.S. 2.01, et seq., Draft Administrative Rules, 14 June 1988.

Wyoming

The state has no cultural resource law with respect to burials or grave goods. Its preservation statute (36-1-114) prohibits excavation of archaeological resources on public land without benefit of a permit issued by the state Board of Land Commissioners. It does not apply to private property and violators incur a penalty of from $25 to $100 and imprisonment for up to six months.

Apparently, the general statutes prohibiting desecration of graves and bodies (6-4-501, 6-4-502) and use of dead bodies (35-4-603) do not apply to prehistoric aboriginal remains. However, the office of the attorney general has not issued an opinion on this issue (Carlson 1989). The practice is for all disturbed Indian burials to be referred to the county coroner's office, which may establish its own rules (Carlson 1989). Infrequently, the coroner will seek direction from the state Historical Preservation Office, but this is reported to be the exception (Marceau 1989).

Clearly, the state legislature has not yet specifically considered an ordering of priorities between the competing values in the issue of appropriate disposition of prehistoric aboriginal remains and grave goods. However, the practice by the archaeologists and physical anthropologists at the University of Wyoming may be more sensitive to aboriginal concerns. By published policy, the university's department of anthropology states an intent to coordinate closely with elected leaders of Indian tribes all cases involving Indian remains of known or suspected affinity with any of the tribes. Further, the department will not excavate unthreatened or undisturbed burial sites, though it will participate in salvage operations (Gill and Frison n.d.).

Statutes

Wyo. Stat. 6-4-501, 6-4-502, Desecrating Graves and Bodies.
Wyo. Stat. 35-4-602, Disposal of Unclaimed Human Bodies.
Wyo. Stat. 36-1-114, Protection of Prehistoric Ruins, etc.

5 Conclusion

Horowitz (1985:xi, 681) stresses the importance of establishing a general understanding of the elements and processes of interethnic conflict. In studying interethnic interaction, Barth advocates beginning at the point where the players and issues most openly interact (1981:83). The current aboriginal social dynamic involves a vast complex of elements, including enculturation, national and global network formation, value formation, interethnic conflict, creation of tradition and ethnic identity, factionalization, and various modes of dispute resolution.

In the United States, as in Australia and Canada, the issue of appropriate disposition of aboriginal remains and grave goods has become a nexus point at which many of these processes intersect. Aboriginal efforts employ means perceived as legitimate by the European-American society: recourse through employment of formal law. These efforts are publicized and often published, and competing values and participants involved in the dispute are presented fully and publicly. Analysis of the processes, with law as the point of entry to the study, should provide useful insight into the complex social dynamics at work. Data obtained in such an investigation may apply to other situations of ethnic conflict and interaction and to other issues arising from aboriginal social dynamics in the United States.

Law is a social construct that reflects both modal values held by a population and the relative ordering of those values. Law, especially common law, tends to be directional and is a product of the disputes and problems presented to it historically. It is not immutable, but neither is it greatly flexible.

When law is confronted with new situations that it previously has not had the opportunity to consider, seemingly bizarre and anomalous legal resolutions can occur. If such resolutions offend the host population's modal sense of ordering of competing values, the law will be changed, usually through statutory reform. New laws are perceived to be required to solve new problems.

From the perspective of the social activist representing a minority group, effecting statutory change requires recruiting the support of the majority population or at least convincing a majority of the legislators that such support has been obtained. The effort may employ consciousness-raising techniques to sensitize the larger population to the specific values underlying the changes sought. The attempt is more likely to be successful if appeal can be made to dormant values already held by the majority population than through the promotion of new or alien values. Such techniques may also denigrate or obscure values in competition with those values promoted by the activists.

Relevant United States law developed from a foundation of English common law that would not have been sympathetic to aboriginal demands had those demands been presented to the courts of the time. No reason exists to expect that aboriginal decedents would have been granted greater legal protection than the minimal protection provided to members of the larger population. As American common law and early statutory law developed, it was deprived of the experiential base of problems related to aboriginal funerary practices, property rights, descent and distribution, and other exigencies of everyday life. This deprivation was a result of the isolation of aboriginal communities from European-American society, racial bias and confiscatory behavior by European-American institutions, and the competency of aboriginal tribunals in dealing with aboriginal problems.

Thus, statutory and common law regimes generally developed in a manner that preserved elements of the European-American experience, such as dedicated cemeteries, marked burials, and priority for the integrity of private property, all of which led to limited definitions of standing. Later, after exposure to acculturation processes, aboriginal claimants presented demands at court for the protection of the remains of decedents alleged to be their ancestors. Consideration of traditional aboriginal mortuary practices—unmarked burials and cemeteries, for instance—presented new problems with which the established laws were ill equipped to deal. Paradoxical decisions arose, such as the declarations that traditional aboriginal cemeteries holding the remains of several hundred individuals did not constitute legal cemeteries and that prehistoric aboriginal skeletons did not constitute bodies or corpses. In response, new legislation began to appear to remedy the perceived inequities.

Federal laws designed to preserve aboriginal sites and remains originated in 1906 with the Antiquities Act. A succession of laws were enacted subsequently that progressively gave greater protection to remains and greater consideration to aboriginal sensitivities. Not until 1989, with passage of the National Museum of the the American Indian Act, and 1990, with enactment of the American Graves Protection and Repatriation Act, did those laws view prehistoric aboriginal remains and grave goods other than as a form of property, and the predominant emphasis was on preservation and not on repatriation or reburial of remains or grave goods. Policies of federal agencies have gone further with these considerations than all but the most recent statutes, to the extent that the new reburial and preservation policy of the U.S. Forest Service is reported to have created controversy among the agencies and is alleged to be inconsistent with the Archaeological Resources Protection Act.

As of August, 1989, twenty-seven states had enacted legislation specifically protective of aboriginal remains. Others provide extensive protection under their desecration and cemetery laws. Some do neither. The variety in approach and treatment is vast, and there is little utility, and some risk of confusion, in attempting to generalize categories of treatment at law.

The practical impact of the laws cannot be assessed until the actual administration of them has been observed. Most state laws are new, as are the strongest of the federal laws, and in many cases implementing regulations have not yet been drafted. The clear trend is toward greater consideration of aboriginal concerns. In fact, of the twenty-seven states possessing specific legislation, twenty-two have made provision for consultation with aboriginal groups during the decision-making process. The opportunity for such participation is an important aboriginal objective. The appendix provides a general descriptive overview of some salient features of the legal regime in each state. This chart is an updated and slightly expanded version of the chart that first appeared in Ubelaker and Grant (1989:275).

The presence of legislation does not necessarily determine the degree of respectful treatment given remains. For example, statutes in Florida and North Carolina are reported to fall short of their intended objectives. States without specific legislation, such as Alabama and Alaska, are sometimes reported to have achieved success in ensuring respectful treatment of remains. The least contentious situations appear to occur in states where the administration (e.g., the state historical-preservation officer or the state archaeologist), the major museums and universities, and the resident Indian population have established cooperative and enlightened relationships regarding these issues, with or without benefit of statutory mandate. There are at least three common elements contributing to failure in operative effect of the specific statutes: factionalization among residential aboriginal communities, inadequate funding of preservation programs on the part of the state legislatures, and a lack of support given to enforcement of the laws by the resident professional community.

Reliable prediction of the future course of the law is elusive. In part, the directions will be a function of society's ranking of the values that eventually are seen to compete with reburial and repatriation, and the efficacy with which these values are presented to the general public by those who promote them. Competing values held by the majority population include the integrity of private property, the advancement of science and education, the stand against taking property without compensation, and possibly the principle of maintaining separation of church and state. An even more significant obstacle might be concern over the cost of the preservation programs.

If the argument prevails that interference with commercial use of private property occasioned by some of the state statutes requires compensation by the state to the landowner, the cost to the public will be enormous. Even the cost of administering reburial programs is more than initially anticipated by some state legislatures. Practical experience gained from living with the new laws, as with most new laws, probably will result in modifications of them—legislators are rarely prescient. The U.S. Supreme Court is likely to be the ultimate arbiter of the constitutional issues now raised in the state courts.

Barth (1981:85) suggests that through time the priorities of competing groups will become more consistent with one another. Thus, attitudes and demands of the participants may gradually converge as the negotiation process continues, lessening the extremity of demands presented by each side and achieving an equilibrium.

Appendix
Tabular Summary
of State Legislation

Appendix
Tabular Summary of State Legislation

	Alabama	Alaska	Arizona	Arkansas	California	Colorado	Connecticut	Delaware	Florida	Georgia
1. Does the state have an aborigine-oriented reburial or unmarked graves law?	no	no	no	—	yes	no	yes	yes	yes	no
2. Does the law require reburial of skeletal remains discovered prospectively?	—	—	—	—	yes	—	yes	yes	yes	—
3. Does the law require reburial of skeletal remains and associated artifacts discovered prospectively?	—	—	—	—	yes	—	no	no	yes	—
4. Does the law require retroactive reburial of skeletal remains from existing scientific or educational collections?	—	—	—	—	no	—	no	yes	no	—
5. Does the law require retroactive reburial of skeletal remains and associated artifacts from existing scientific or educational collections?	—	—	—	—	no	—	no	no	no	—
6. Do the state's general laws offer protection of aboriginal remains?	?	yes	yes	—	—	yes	yes	—	yes	?
7. Does the law provide for aboriginal participation in decision making?	no	yes	yes	—	yes	no	yes	yes	yes	no

This table, accurate as of August 1989, is an updated and slightly expanded modification of one that first appeared in Ubelaker and Grant (1989:275).

Hawaii	Idaho	Illinois	Indiana	Iowa	Kansas	Kentucky	Louisiana	Maine	Maryland	Massachusetts	Michigan	Minnesota	Mississippi	Missouri	Montana	Nebraska	Nevada	New Hampshire	New Jersey
yes	yes	yes	yes	yes	yes	no	no	yes	no	yes	no	yes	yes	yes	no	yes	yes	yes	no
yes	yes	no	yes	yes	yes	—	—	yes	—	yes	—	yes	—	yes	—	yes	yes	yes	—
no	yes	no	?	no	yes	—	—	no	—	no	—	no	—	no	—	yes	yes	no	—
no	no	no	no	no	no	—	—	no	—	no	—	yes	—	no	—	yes	yes	no	—
no	no	no	no	no	no	—	—	no	—	no	—	no	—	no	—	yes	—	no	—
—	yes	no	yes	—	—	yes	yes	—	yes	yes	yes	yes	yes	yes	?	—	—	—	?
yes	yes	no	?	yes	yes	no	no	no	no	yes	no	yes	no	yes	no	yes	yes	yes	no

	New Mexico	New York	North Carolina	North Dakota	Ohio	Oklahoma	Oregon	Pennsylvania	Rhode Island	South Carolina
1. Does the state have an aborigine-oriented reburial or unmarked graves law?	yes	no	yes	yes	no	yes	yes	no	no	no
2. Does the law require reburial of skeletal remains discovered prospectively?	?	—	yes	yes	—	yes	yes	—	—	—
3. Does the law require reburial of skeletal remains and associated artifacts discovered prospectively?	no	—	no	yes	—	yes	yes	—	—	—
4. Does the law require retroactive reburial of skeletal remains from existing scientific or educational collections?	no	—	no	no	—	no	no	—	—	—
5. Does the law require retroactive reburial of skeletal remains and associated artifacts from existing scientific or educational collections?	no	—	no	no	—	no	no	—	—	—
6. Do the state's general laws offer protection of aboriginal remains?	yes	?	yes	yes	?	—	—	yes	yes	yes
7. Does the law provide for aboriginal participation in decision making?	no	no	yes	yes	no	yes	yes	no	no	no

South Dakota	Tennessee	Texas	Utah	Vermont	Virginia	Washington	West Virginia	Wisconsin	Wyoming
no	yes	no	no	no	yes	yes	no	yes	no
—	yes	—	—	—	no	yes	—	no	—
—	no	—	—	—	no	yes	—	yes	—
—	no	—	—	—	no	no	—	no	—
—	no	—	—	—	no	no	—	no	—
yes	yes	?	yes	yes	yes	yes	yes	—	no
no	no	no	no	no	no	yes	?	yes	no

Works Cited

Adams, Lloyd. 1989a. Letter to author, 8 May.

Adams, Robert M. 1989b. "Bones of Contention." Letters, *Harper's*, April.

Alex, Robert. 1986. "Archaeology Special: American Indian Skeletal Remains Reburied." *History Notes* (South Dakota State Historical Society) 1 (4): 5–6.

Anonymous. n.d. "What to Do upon Encountering Human Remains." Publication of the New Hampshire Division of Historical Resources.

———. 1982. "Policy Manual for the Museum of New Mexico" (1 July). Santa Fe: New Mexico Office of Cultural Affairs.

———. 1986. "Grave Robbing Nets Fine, Probation; Tribe Angered." *Lewiston Morning Tribune* (Idaho), 5 June.

———. 1987. "Indian Cemetery: Peace in Delaware." *New York Times*, 12 July.

———. 1989a. *Historical Newsletter of the Nebraska State Historical Society* 4 (18): 2.

———. 1989b. "Supplemental Note on House Bill No. 2144." Kansas Legislative Research Department. Topeka.

———. 1989c. "Coahoma Jails 3 for Desecration of Indian Site." *Clarksdale Clarion-Ledger* (Mississippi), 11 January.

Arden, Harvey. 1989. "Who Owns Our Past?" *National Geographic* 175 (March): 376–92.

Arnold, Donald C. (Oregon Chief Counsel). 1988. Opinion OP-6275 to Division of State Lands, 14 October.

Ashworth, Treva (South Carolina Assistant Attorney General). 1987. Opinion letter to South Carolina Institute of Archaeology and Anthropology, 26 August.

Austin, Richard H. (Michigan Secretary of State). 1986. Letter to Frank J. Kelley (Michigan Attorney General), 6 February.

Barth, Fredrik. 1981. *Process and Form in Social Life*. London: Rutledge and Kegan Paul.

Bates, Badger. 1989. "Aborigines, Archaeologists, and the Rights of the Dead." Paper presented at the World Archaeological Congress, Vermillion, South Dakota, 8 August.

Bloemker, Jim. [1989]. Letter to author, received 11 March, 1989.

Bohannon, Paul. 1965. "The Differing Realms of the Law." In *The Ethnography of Law*, special publication of *American Anthropologist* 67:33–42.

Bowman, Margaret B. 1989. "The Reburial of Native American Skeletal Remains: Approaches to the Resolution of a Conflict." *Harvard Environmental Law Review* 13:147–208.

Brace, C. Loring. 1988. "A Dental Anthropological Perspective on the Amerindian Reburial Issue." *Dental Anthropology Newsletter* 3 (3): 1–4.

Bradley, Robert L. (Member, Maine Historic Preservation Commission). 1989. Letter to author, 12 April.

Brookes, Stephen. 1988. "Indians Gaining on the U.S. in Battle over Ancestral Bones." *Insight*, 10 October, 20–22.

Brooks, Robert L. 1988. "Management and Treatment of Burial Remains: An Oklahoma Perspective." Paper presented at the Fifty-third Annual Meeting of the Society for American Archaeology, Phoenix, Arizona.

Brooms, McDonald. 1989. Letter to author, 26 April.

Buford, Cathy (Arkansas State Historical Preservation Officer). 1989. Letter to author, 14 April.

Buikstra, Jane E. 1981. "A Specialist in Ancient Cemetery Studies Looks at the Reburial Issue." *Early Man* 32:26–27.

Byrd, Kathleen (Louisiana State Archaeologist). 1989a. Letter to author, 22 March.

———. 1989b. Telephone interview, 5 July.

Carlson, Criss (Staff Attorney, Office of Wyoming Attorney General). 1989. Letter to author, 24 February.

Carvell, Charles M. (North Dakota Assistant Attorney General). 1989. Letter to author, 19 July.

Christensen, Diana. 1989. Letter to author, 11 April.

Claggett, Stephen R. (North Carolina Chief Archaeologist). 1988. "Pragmatic Aspects of Skeletal Reinterment: The North Carolina Experience." Paper presented at the Fifty-third Annual Meeting of the Society for American Archaeology, Phoenix, Arizona.

———. 1989. Letter to author, 20 April.

Clouse, Janet M. (Colorado Assistant Attorney General). 1979. Opinion letter to state archaeologist, 1 March.

Cohen, Felix S. 1942. *Handbook of Federal Indian Law*. Reprint. Albuquerque: Five Rings Corporation, 1986.

Cole, Elizabeth J. 1989. Letter to author, 27 April.

Collier, Jane F. 1975. "Legal Processes." In *Annual Review of Anthropology*, edited by Bernard J. Siegel et al. Palo Alto, Calif.: Annual Reviews.

Comaroff, John L., and Simon Roberts. 1981. *Rules and Processes* Chicago: University of Chicago Press.

Crazy Horse, Roy. 1989. Telephone interview, 19 March.

Davis, Tom G. (Texas Assistant Attorney General). 1989. Opinion letter LO-89-7 to executive director of the Texas Historical Commission, 30 January.

Deloria, Vine, Jr. 1973. *God is Red.* New York: Grosset and Dunlap.

———. 1974. *Custer Died for Your Sins: An Indian Manifesto.* New York: Macmillan.

Denney, Shawn W. 1981. Informal letter opinion to Illinois Division of Historic Sites, 7 May.

Devine, Michael. 1986. "Policy on Disposition of Archaeological and Historic Human Remains" (October). Springfield: Illinois Historic Preservation Agency.

Di Pasquale, Nick (Missouri House Research Analyst). n.d. "SB 24: Unmarked Human Burial Sites."

Disse, Diane. 1987. "Museums, Historical Societies, and Issues Related to Native American Culture." News release of the Minnesota Historical Society, 28 September.

Dobyns, Henry F., and Robert C. Euler. 1967. *The Ghost Dance of 1889.* Prescott, Ariz.: Prescott College Press.

Driver, Harold E. 1969. *Indians of North America.* 2d ed. Chicago: University of Chicago Press.

Dunn, Robert E., Jr. (New Hampshire Assistant Attorney General). 1988. Opinion letter to state archaeologist, 10 November.

———. 1989. Letter to author, 6 March.

Echo-Hawk, Walter R. 1985. "Sacred Material and the Law." Paper presented at the Plains Indian Museum's Ninth Annual Plains Indian Seminar: The Concept of Sacred Materials and Their Place in the World. Cody, Wyoming, 27–29 September.

———. 1986. "Museum Rights vs. Indian Rights: Guidelines for Assessing Competing Legal Interests in Native Cultural Resources." *New York University Journal of Law and Social Change* 14:437–53.

———. 1988. "Tribal Efforts to Protect against Mistreatment of Indian Dead: The Quest for Equal Protection of the Laws." *NARF Legal Review* 14:1–5.

Ellis, Chet. 1988. "An American Indian Perspective: Missouri's Unmarked Human Burials or Remains, RSMo. 194.400–410." Paper presented at the Joint Annual Meeting of the Kansas Anthropological Association and the Missouri Archaeological Society, Overland Park, Kansas, 17 April.

Fielder, Nick. 1989. "Tennessee's Archaeological and Cemetery Laws." Paper for the Tennessee Division of Archaeology, Nashville, Tennessee, 25 January.

Fimbel, Deborah R. 1988. Untitled paper presented at the Mid-Atlantic Archaeological Conference, Rehobeth, Maryland, 25 March.

Fineman, Martha L. 1986. "Illusive Equality: On Weitzman's Divorce Revolution." *American Bar Association Research Journal* 4 (Fall): 781–90.

Frazier, Bill. 1988. "Unmarked Human Remains." *Profile* 63:3.

Frizzell, Kent. 1974. "Foreword. Evolution of Jurisdiction in Indian Country." *University of Kansas Law Review* 22:341–49.

Funk, Karen J. 1989. "Native Spirits and Congress: Moving toward a Federally Mandated Reburial Congress." Paper presented at the World Archaeological Congress, Vermillion, South Dakota, 9 August.

Gill, George W., and George C. Frison. n.d. "Excavation and Handling of Human Remains." Policy statement of the Department of Anthropology, University of Wyoming, Laramie.

Gill, Sam D. 1983. *Native American Traditions.* Belmont, Calif.: Wadsworth.

Goldman, Nathan. 1989. Letter to the director of the Kentucky Heritage Council, 3 May.

Goodenough, Ward H. 1964. Introduction to *Explorations in Cultural Anthropology*, edited by Ward H. Goodenough. New York: McGraw-Hill.

Gorospe, Kathy. 1985. *American Indian Cultural Resources: A Preservation Handbook.* Salem, Mass.: Commission on Indian Services.

Green, William. n.d. "Protection of Ancient Burials in Iowa" (brochure). Iowa City: Office of the State Archaeologist of Iowa.

Greenberg, Joseph H., C. G. Turner, and S. L. Zegura. 1986. "The Settlement of the Americas: A Comparison of the Linguistic, Dental, and Genetic Evidence." *Current Anthropology* 27:477–97.

Griffin, Annie (Archaeologist, Hawaii Department of Land and Natural Resources). 1989. Telephone interview, 29 June.

Halsey, John R. (Michigan State Archaeologist). 1986. Memorandum to the director of the Michigan Bureau of History, 7 February.

———. 1989. Letter to author, 12 April.

Hammil, Jan. 1988. Unpublished transcript of the Society for American Archaeology Special Event "Reburial," Phoenix, Arizona, 1 April.

Hanson, James A. 1989. "From the Director." *Historical Newsletter of the Nebraska State Historical Society* 41 (8): 1.

Heizer, Robert F. 1974. "A Question of Ethics in Archaeology: One Archaeologist's View." *Journal of California Archaeology* 1 (2): 145–51.

Hertzberg, Hazel W. 1973. "Pan-Indianism." In *The American Indian: A*

Rising Ethnic Force, edited by Herbert L. Marx, Jr. New York: H. W. Wilson.

Higginbotham, C. Dean. 1982. "Native Americans versus Archaeologists: The Legal Issues." *American Indian Law Review* 10:91–115.

Hillinger, Charles. 1988. "Bulldozers Destroy Clues to Nevada's Past." *Express*, 22 October.

Hobsbawm, Eric. 1985. *The Invention of Tradition*. Cambridge: Cambridge University Press.

Hoebel, E. Adamson. 1954. *The Law of Primitive Man*. Cambridge: Harvard University Press. Reprint. New York: Atheneum, 1983.

———. 1972. *Anthropology: The Study of Man*. 4th ed. New York: McGraw-Hill.

Horowitz, Donald L. 1985. *Ethnic Groups in Conflict*. Berkeley: University of California Press.

Hubert, Jane. 1989. "A Proper Place for the Dead: A Critical Review of the 'Reburial' Issue." In *Conflict in the Archaeology of Living Traditions*, edited by R. Layton. London: Unwin Hyman.

Humphrey, Hubert H., III (Minnesota Attorney General). 1989. Letter to author, 25 April.

Israel, Benjamin. 1989. "Builder Destroys Indian Burial Sites." *Columbia Daily Tribune*, 14 April.

Kalima, Patricia. 1989. "Victory is Hollow." *Maui News*, 2 March.

Karus, Linda A. 1989. Letter to author, 1 May.

Kay, Paul. 1966. "Ethnography and Theory of Culture." *Bucknell Review* 19:106–13.

Kearney, Michael. 1984. *World View*. Novato, Calif.: Chandler and Sharp.

Keesing, Roger M. 1976. *Cultural Anthropology: A Contemporary Perspective*. New York: Holt, Rinehart and Winston.

Keller, Renee M. 1989. Letter to author, 19 April.

Kelley, Frank J. (Michigan Attorney General). 1989. Opinion 6585, to Richard H. Austin (Michigan Secretary of State), June 7.

King, Thomas F., Patricia P. Hickman, and Gary Berg. 1977. *Anthropology in Historic Preservation*. New York: Academic Press.

Kroeber, A.L. 1948. *Anthropology*. New York: Harcourt, Brace and World.

Kwanashie, Patrick B. (Connecticut Assistant Attorney General). 1989. Letter to author, 8 March.

Lees, William B. 1988. "Current Status of the Kansas Unmarked Human Burial and Skeletal Remains Protection Act." Paper presented at the Joint Annual Meeting of the Kansas Anthropological Association and the Missouri Archaeological Society, Overland Park, Kansas, 17 April.

Lewin, Roger. 1984. "Extinction Threatens Australian Anthropology." *Science*, 225:393–94.

Lurie, Nancy O. 1971a. "An American Indian Renascence?" In *The American Indian Today*, edited by Stuart Levine and Nancy O. Lurie. De Land, Fla.: Everett/Edwards.

———. 1971b. "The Contemporary American Indian Scene." In *North American Indians in Historical Perspective*, edited by Eleanor B. Leacock and Nancy O. Lurie. New York: Random House.

———. 1986. "Money, Semantics, and Indian Leadership." *American Indian Quarterly* 10:47–63.

McCarthy, John P. 1984. "Provisional Draft Guidelines for Archaeological Investigations in Cultural Resources Management." New Jersey Department of Environmental Protection, 12 March.

McGahey, Samuel O. n.d. "Legal Protection of Aboriginal Burials in Mississippi." Memorandum to the Mississippi Department of Archives and History.

McGuire, Randall H. 1989. "The Sanctity of the Grave: White Concepts and American Indian Burials." In *Conflict in the Archaeology of Living Traditions*, edited by R. Layton. London: Unwin Hyman.

Madsen, David B. 1989. Telephone interview, 11 April.

Marceau, Thomas E. (Wyoming Department State Historical Preservation Officer). 1989. Letter to author, 19 April.

Marx, Herbert L., Jr. 1973. *The American Indian: A Rising Ethnic Force*. New York: H. W. Wilson.

Mason, Alicia (New Mexico Assistant Attorney General). 1987. Opinion letter 87–31, to director of the Museum of New Mexico, 15 July.

Mathews, Jay. 1989. "University to Return Ancestral Bones to Tribe." *Washington Post*, 23 June.

Meighan, Clement W. 1984. "Archaeology: Science or Sacrilege?" In *Ethics and Values in Archaeology*, edited by Ernestine L. Green. New York: Free Press, 208–23.

———. 1986. *Archaeology and Anthropological Ethics*. Calabasas, Calif.: Wormwood Press.

Mercado-Allinger, Pat. 1989. Letter to author, 24 April.

Merryman, John H. 1986. "Who Owns the Elgin Marbles?" *Artnews*, 85: 100–109.

Mertz, Douglas K. (Alaska Assistant Attorney General). 1989. Letter to author, 23 February.

Mixon, Jeff (Oklahoma Assistant Attorney General). 1989. Letter to author, 16 February.

Moore, Michael C. 1989. "The Tennessee State Cemetery Law and Its Impact upon Prehistoric Site Preservation." Paper presented at the Fifty-fourth Annual Meeting of the Society for American Archaeology, Atlanta, Georgia, 5–9 April.

Moore, Steve. 1987. "Federal Indian Burial Policy: Historical Anachronism or Contemporary Reality?" *NARF Legal Review* 12:1–7.

Moreland, Jerre William. 1989. "American Indian Socialization into the Legal Profession: A Preliminary Ethnography." Paper presented at the Annual Meeting of the Law and Society Association, Madison, Wisconsin, June 9.

Morenon, E. Pierre. 1987. "Archaeological Site or Human Cemetery? The Players, Rules, and Strategy for Studying Places in Rhode Island." Paper presented at Symposium: The Reburial Issue in the Northeast, Amherst, Massachusetts, 19 March.

Nader, Laura. 1965. "The Anthropological Study of Law." *The Ethnography of Law*, special publication of *American Anthropologist* 67:3–32.

Nagata, Ralston H. (Hawaii State Historical Preservation Officer). 1989. Letter to author, 25 April.

Neusius, Sarah W. 1989. Letter to author, 22 June.

Newcomb, William W., Jr. 1974. *North American Indians: An Anthropological Perspective*. Pacific Palisades, Calif.: Goodyear.

O'Brien, Sharon. 1988. "A History of the American Indian Religious Freedom Act and Its Implementation." *Indian Affairs* 116:ii–x.

Olson, James S., and Raymond Wilson. 1984. *Native Americans in the Twentieth Century*. Provo, Utah: Brigham University Press.

Pascoe, Fay N. (Mississippi Assistant Attorney General). 1978. Opinion to Samuel O. McGahey (State Historical Preservation Officer), 5 October.

Perry, Kate M. 1985. "Federal Preservation Law." In *Historic Preservation Law and Tax Planning for Old and Historic Buildings*. Philadelphia: American Law Institute.

Poirier, David A., et al. 1985. "Native American Burials in Connecticut: The Ethical, Scientific, and Bureaucratic Matrix." *Bulletin of the Archaeological Society of Connecticut* 48:3–12.

Pollack, David (Archaeologist, Kentucky State Historic Preservation Office). 1989. Letter to author, 24 April.

Pospisil, Leopold. 1968. "Law and Order." In *Introduction to Cultural Anthropology*, edited by James A. Clifton. Boston: Houghton Mifflin.

Potter, Parker B., Jr. (New Hampshire Research Archaeologist). 1989. Letter to author, 12 April.

Powell, Mary L. 1989. "Salvage Bioarchaeology: Coping with Commingled Human Remains from a Looted Site." Paper presented at the Fifty-eighth Annual Meeting of the American Association of Physical Anthropologists, San Diego, California, 4–8 April.

Preston, Douglas J. 1989. "Skeletons in Our Museums' Closets." *Harper's*, February, 66.

Price, H. Marcus, III. 1988. "Bones of Contention: Reburial of Human Remains under RS Mo. 194.400–.410." *Missouri Archaeological Society Quarterly* 5:4–18.

———. 1989a. "State Reburial Statutes and Inverse Condemnation." *Missouri Archaeological Society Quarterly* 6 (4): 8.

———. 1989b. "An Overview of the State Reburial Laws in Practice." Paper presented at the World Archaeological Congress, Vermillion, South Dakota, 7 August.

Quick, Polly M., ed. 1985. *Proceedings: Conference on Reburial Issues.* Chicago: Newberry Library.

Raber, Paul A. 1985. "A Comprehensive State Plan for the Conservation of Archaeological Resources." Harrisburg: Pennsylvania Historical and Museum Commission.

Rathbun, Ted A. 1989. Letter to author, 17 April.

Riggs, Rodney. 1989. "The Burial Site Preservation Program in Wisconsin." Paper presented at the Annual Meeting of the Society for American Archaeology, Phoenix, Arizona, 28 April.

Roberson, Jan. 1988. "Compromise Sought in Remains' Location." *Lahaina News*, 7 December.

Roberts, Daniel G. 1984. "Management and Community Aspects of the Excavation of a Sensitive Urban Archaeological Resource: An Example from Philadelphia." *American Archaeology* 4:235–40.

Roberts, John M. 1964. "The Self-Management of Cultures." In *Explorations in Cultural Anthropology*, edited by Ward H. Goodenough. New York: McGraw-Hill.

Robinson, William J., and Roderick Sprague. 1965. "Disposal of the Dead at Point of Pines, Arizona." *American Antiquity* 30:442–53.

Rogers, Everett M. 1971. *Communication of Innovations.* 2d ed. New York: Free Press.

Rosen, Lawrence. 1980. "The Excavation of American Indian Burial Sites: A Problem in Law and Professional Responsibility." *American Anthropologist* 82:5–27.

Ross, Dick. 1988. "The Bandon Case: Applying the Oregon Reburial Law." Paper provided by Oregon Department of Parks and Recreation, Corvallis, Oregon.

Scarry, John. 1989. Letter to author, 18 April.

Schneider, Kent A., Gordon R. Peters, and Russell Kaldenberg. 1988. "Treatment of Human Remains: A Policy." Paper presented at the Annual Meeting of the Society for American Archaeology, Phoenix, Arizona, 28 April.

Schneider, Kent A., and Michael R. Beckes. 1989. "Reinterment and the Treatment of Human Remains: Working at Consensus in the Real World." Paper presented at Symposium: CRM in the 1990's, American Society for Conservation Archaeology, Atlanta, Georgia, 8 April.

Schneider, Michael H. 1989. "Preliminary Notes: Protecting Burials under the Common Law." Memorandum, Albuquerque, New Mexico.

Schwab, David. 1989. Telephone interview, 29 March.

Simon, Brona G. n.d. "An Analysis of the Massachusetts Unmarked Burial Law." Paper for the Massachusetts Historical Commission, Boston.

——. 1988. "An Evaluation of the Results and Archaeological Benefits of the Implementation of the Unmarked Burial Law in Massachusetts." Paper presented at the Annual Meeting of the Society for American Archaeology, Phoenix, Arizona, 28 April.

Simon, Brona G., and Valerie A. Talmage. 1989. "The Status of State Programs Protecting Burial Sites in New England." *CNEA Newsletter* 8 (2): 3–12.

Slusher, M. Catherine (Virginia State Archaeologist). 1989. Telephone interview, 11 April.

Smith, Frederick H. 1984. "Legal Aspects and Suggested Protocol in Dealing with Human Remains Found in an Archaeological Context in Alaska." *Arctic Anthropology* 21:141–47.

Sobol, Thomas. 1989. "An Invitation for Comment." Albany: New York State Education Department.

Spaeth, Nicholas J. (North Dakota Attorney General). 1989. Opinion letter to the superintendent of the State Historical Society, July 7.

Spire, Robert M. (Nebraska Attorney General). 1988. Opinion letter to the executive director of the Nebraska Indian Commission, 14 December.

Starr, June, and Jane F. Collier. 1987. "Historical Studies of Legal Change." *Current Anthropology* 28:367–72.

Sutton, Imre. 1985. Prolegomena to *Unredeemable America*, edited by Imre Sutton. Albuquerque: University of New Mexico Press.

Thompson, Raymond. 1986. "Museums and the Treatment of Human Remains." Paper presented at the Annual Meeting of the Society for American Archaeology, New Orleans, Louisiana, 24 April.

Tomsho, Robert. 1989. "Indian Burial Site Becomes Big Issue in Little Salina, Kansas." *Wall Street Journal,* 17 May.

Trigger, Bruce G. 1980. "Archaeology and the Image of the American Indian." *American Antiquity* 45:662–75.

Turpen, Michael C. (Oklahoma Attorney General). 1986. Opinion 86-43, to the executive director of the Oklahoma State Historical Society, 24 November.

Ubelaker, Douglas H., and Lauryn G. Grant. 1989. "Human Skeletal Remains: Preservation or Reburial?" *Yearbook of Physical Anthropology* 32:248–87.

Walker, Deward E., Jr. 1972. *The Emergent Native Americans*. Boston: Little, Brown.

———. 1989. "Testimony in Support of LB 340." Testimony before the Nebraska General Assembly, Lincoln, 25 January.

Wallace, Anthony F. C. 1970. *Culture and Personality*. 2d ed. New York: Random House.

Wax, Murray L. 1971. *Indian Americans: Unity and Diversity*. Englewood Cliffs, N.J.: Prentice-Hall.

White, Marvin L., Jr. (Mississippi Assistant Attorney General). 1980. Opinion to E. Hilliard (Director of Department of Archives and History), 12 September.

Wilker, William H. 1989. Letter to author, 9 March.

Willey, Gordon R., and Jeremy A. Sabloff. 1980. *A History of American Archaeology*. 2d ed. San Francisco: W. H. Freeman.

Williams, Joyce A. (Illinois Staff Archaeologist). 1989. Letter to author, 21 April.

Wilson, Paul E., and Elaine O. Zingg. 1974. "What is America's Heritage? Historic Preservation and American Indian Culture." *University of Kansas Law Review* 22:413–53.

Worsely, Peter. 1959. "Cargo Cults." *Scientific American* 200:117–206.

Yudien, Geoffrey A. (Vermont Assistant Attorney General). 1989. Letter to author, 28 February.

Zimmerman, Larry J. 1981. "Digging Ancient Burials: The Crow Creek Experience." *Early Man* 31:3–10.

———. 1985a. "Desecration and Reburial as an Anthropological Issue: The Tactics of Self-delusion." Paper presented at the Annual Meeting of the American Anthropological Association, Washington, D.C., 4–8 December.

———. 1985b. "A Perspective on the Reburial Issue from South Dakota." Appendix 2 of *Proceedings: Conference on Reburial Issues*, edited by Polly M. Quick. Chicago: Newberry Library.

———. 1989. "Human Bones as Symbols of Power: Aboriginal American Belief Systems toward Bones and 'Grave-robbing' Archaeologists." In *Conflict in the Archaeology of Living Traditions*, edited by Robert Layton. London: Unwin Hyman.